GW00675921

EDITED BY IVAN MESA

BEFORE YOU LOSE

DECONSTRUCTING
DOUBT IN
THE CHURCH

YOUR FAITH

TREVIN WAX · RACHEL GILSON · JAY Y. KIM · BRETT McCRACKEN
KAREN SWALLOW PRIOR · CLAUDE ATCHO · DEREK RISHMAWY
JOSHUA RYAN BUTLER · JARED C. WILSON · AND MORE

Art Direction: Steven Morales
Cover Design: Gabriel Reyes-Ordeix
Illustration: Aaron Schock
Typesetting: Ryan Leichty

ISBN:
978-0-9992843-7-7 (Print)
978-0-9992843-9-1 (Mobi)
978-0-9992843-8-4 (ePub)

Printed in the United States of America

CONTENTS

PART TWO
DECONSTRUCT THE ISSUES

PART THREE
RECONSTRUCT FAITH

CONTRIBUTORS

CLAUDE ATCHO serves as a pastor at Fellowship Memphis, a multi-ethnic church in Memphis, Tennessee. He is the author of a forthcoming book on African American literature and theology with Brazos (spring 2022).

HUNTER BEAUMONT (ThM, Dallas Theological Seminary) is lead pastor of Fellowship Denver Church and serves on the board of Acts 29 U.S. West.

JOSHUA RYAN BUTLER is co-lead pastor of Redemption Church in Tempe, Arizona, and author of *The Skeletons in God's Closet* and *The Pursuing God*.

RACHEL GILSON serves on the leadership team of theological development and culture for Cru. She is the author of *Born Again This Way: Coming Out, Coming to Faith, and What Comes Next* and is pursuing a PhD in public theology at Southeastern Baptist Theological Seminary.

IAN HARBER is the communication director of a local nonprofit in Denton, Texas. He is pursuing his MDiv at The Southern Baptist Theological Seminary and ministers to young adults in his local church.

SAMUEL JAMES is an associate acquisitions editor at Crossway Books, editor of Letter & Liturgy, and contributing editor at The Gospel Coalition.

JAY Y. KIM is lead pastor of teaching at WestGate Church (Silicon Valley, California) and is teacher-in-residence at Vintage Faith (Santa Cruz, California). He's the author of *Analog Church: Why We Need Real People, Places, and Things in the Digital Age*.

JEREMY LINNEMAN is the founding pastor of Trinity Community Church in Columbia, Missouri. He previously served for seven years as a staff pastor of Sojourn Church in Louisville, Kentucky. Jeremy is a DMin student at Covenant Theological Seminary and the author of *Life-Giving Groups*.

BRETT MCCRACKEN is communications director and senior editor at The Gospel Coalition and author of *The Wisdom Pyramid: Feeding Your Soul in a Post-Truth World*. Brett and his wife, Kira, live in Santa Ana, California, with their two sons. They belong to Southlands Church, where Brett serves as an elder.

IVAN MESA (ThM, The Southern Baptist Theological Seminary) is books editor at The Gospel Coalition. He and his wife, Sarah, have three children and live in eastern Georgia.

KEITH PLUMMER (PhD, Trinity Evangelical Divinity School) is dean of the School of Divinity and professor of theology at Cairn University. He teaches a variety of subjects, including apologetics, technology and Christian discipleship, and pastoral counseling.

KAREN SWALLOW PRIOR is research professor of English and Christianity and culture at Southeastern Baptist Theological Seminary. Her most recent book is *On Reading Well: Finding the Good Life in Great Books*.

DEREK RISHMAWY is the Reformed University Fellowship campus minister at University of California Irvine. He co-hosts the Mere Fidelity podcast and is a PhD candidate at Trinity Evangelical Divinity School.

TREVIN WAX (PhD, Southeastern Baptist Theological Seminary) is senior vice president of theology and communications at LifeWay Christian Resources and a visiting professor at Wheaton College. He is the general editor of The Gospel Project and the author of multiple books, including *Rethink Your Self* and *The Multi-Directional Leader*.

THADDEUS WILLIAMS (PhD, Vrije Universiteit, Amsterdam) is an associate professor of systematic theology at Biola University and author of *Reflect: Becoming Yourself by Mirroring the Greatest Person in History* and *Confronting Injustice Without Compromising Truth: 12 Questions Christians Should Ask About Social Justice*. Thaddeus lives in Southern California, with his wife and four children.

JARED C. WILSON is assistant professor of pastoral ministry at Spurgeon College, author-in-residence at Midwestern Baptist Theological Seminary, and director of the pastoral training center at Liberty Baptist Church, all in Kansas City, Missouri. He is general editor of For The Church (ftc.co) and co-host of For the Church Podcast and *Christianity Today*'s Art of Pastoring Podcast. He is the author of over 20 books, including *The Imperfect Disciple* and *The Gospel-Driven Church*.

INTRODUCTION

IVAN MESA

I had never heard of Rhett and Link—the duo behind Good Mythical Morning (their daily YouTube show with more than 16 million subscribers) and Ear Biscuits (their podcast)—until I learned of their public deconstruction story. The two of them—who as of December 2020 are the fourth-highest YouTube earners, making $20 million a year[1]—shared about how they moved from Cru staffers and missionaries to unbelievers—or, as Rhett now describes himself, a "hopeful agnostic." The comedians have for years been a staple in many homes with children and young adults (with videos ranging from "epic" rap battles to testing the world's hottest peppers to getting shot with Nerf guns), so it wasn't surprising that their public announcement unsettled the faith of many.

While deconstruction stories are nothing new in our secular age—for example, Jen Hatmaker still describes herself as a Christian and Joshua Harris doesn't—it seems that for many, traditional Christian

1.   Rupert Neate, "Ryan Kaji, 9, earns $29.5m as this year's highest-paid YouTuber," The Guardian, December 18, 2020, https://www.theguardian.com/technology/2020/dec/18/ryan-kaji-9-earns-30m-as-this-years-highest-paid-youtuber.

faith is increasingly implausible. According to Rhett, "If I don't *have* to believe [Christianity], then why would I?"

Given how prevalent these stories are becoming, we at The Gospel Coalition have asked some of our most trusted writers to address the deconstruction phenomenon from a number of perspectives. If you're trying to make sense of your faith, I hope these chapters will give you perspective, answer questions, or at least help you understand you're not alone. While it might seem like your world is being shaken, perhaps even like you're experiencing a kind of death, we are convinced a more robust, settled faith can exist on the other side.

WHAT IS DECONSTRUCTION?

First, let's define terms. According to one writer, "Deconstruction is the process of systematically dissecting and often rejecting the beliefs you grew up with. Sometimes the Christian will deconstruct all the way to atheism. Some remain there, but others experience a reconstruction. But the type of faith they end up embracing almost never resembles the Christianity they formerly knew."[2]

Over the past several years, attention paid toward deconstruction stories has increased. And the trend extends far beyond the spotlight of well-known Christians with large social-media followings, book deals, and podcasts. It may be that the high-profile cases have normalized unbelief, emboldening ordinary folks to proceed in their own deconstruction journeys. That's one of the ways social media could be accelerating this trend. Whereas 50 years ago it might've been hard to find a "community" of deconstructing Christians (and thus you didn't feel it was a valid social option), now it's easy to find such "community" online, further removing fears or stigmas that might be associated with spiritual deconstruction.

Of course, while technology has influenced some of these social dimensions, at its core this path toward unbelief is nothing new. Jesus himself warned of it: "Because lawlessness will be increased, the love of many will grow cold. But the one who endures to the end will be

2.   Alisa Childers, *Another Gospel?: A Lifelong Christian Seeks Truth in Response to Progressive Christianity* (Carol Stream, IL: Tyndale, 2000), 24.

saved" (Matt. 24:12–13). From Demas (2 Tim. 4:10) to Hymenaeus and Philetus (1 Tim. 1:20; 2 Tim. 2:17), the early church saw many abandon the faith they once professed (1 John 2:19). We should be saddened, but we shouldn't be surprised.

After being rejected by family and by the nation of Israel (Mark 3:20–30), Jesus redefined true spiritual family as those who do God's will (3:35). Why do some believe and others don't? Why do even those who believe sometimes fail to persevere in faith? In the following chapter of Mark's Gospel we read the parable of the sower and the four soils (4:1–20). Only one out of the four soils produces fruit. Here we learn several important things about the gospel, faith in Jesus, and varying responses to the gospel. Relevant for our discussion, it explains why some who profess faith ultimately fall away. It's a warning for anyone who claims the name of Christ.

But your story, unlike these sober warnings, can end in settled hope and newfound joy.

LOOK TO JESUS

Because you're reading this book, you're likely seeking to make sense of your faith—if Jesus is worth trusting, if it's your own faith and not just some inherited belief system, if there are too many problematic or perplexing issues with Scripture, if it's worth putting up with the failures and hypocrisy of so many who claim the name of Christ. Perhaps these concerns have only exacerbated your doubts, with so many to count that you don't even know where to begin.

Maybe you look around at the contemporary church landscape and think, *This can't be what Jesus had in mind*. Perhaps you've observed a version of cultural Christianity that has more to do with the American Dream than Jesus of Nazareth.

In many times and in many places, believers have struggled with the disappointing fact that not everything calling itself "Christian" resembles the character of Christ and the testimony of the historic church. We'll always see cultural expressions of Christianity that may be more or less biblical. And we'll always be rightly frustrated by this disconnect—sometimes to the point of wanting to disassociate from the mess altogether.

Perhaps you come from a community that didn't live out the Bible. Or perhaps you've not yet found a community where the gospel actually seems alive and real. We want this book to introduce to you a community of believers who've wrestled through these struggles, helped others amid their doubts, and have maybe even experienced deconstruction themselves. Because Christianity—to be more specific, Jesus—can help, whatever your questions. Whatever your struggle, it gets better with more—not less—Christianity. It might be tempting to leave the church in order to find the answers. But we want you to reconsider the church as the best place to deal with your doubts and deconstruction.

Deconstructing, however jarring and emotionally exhausting, need not end in a cul-de-sac of unbelief. In fact, deconstructing can be the road toward reconstructing—building up a more mature, robust faith that grapples honestly with the deepest questions of life. As you read, we pray that Jesus would be more precious to you; that the church, though filled with shortcomings and sins, would welcome and point you to him; and that on the other side of this process, you too would glory in your Savior as you tell others of his never-failing love.

PART ONE

DECONSTRUCT DECONSTRUCTION

1

DOUBT YOUR WAY BACK TO TRUTH

TREVIN WAX

Whenever I hear of someone leaving the church (this time for good!) amid a growing number of doubts about the Christian faith, I'm usually not surprised. I'm sad, but not shocked. In a secular age, I expect people of different faiths and those who claim no faith at all to wrestle with various questions and doubts. It's less surprising to me when someone succumbs to the subtle pull of secularism than when people maintain a firm conviction that their religion is true, not merely helpful.

This kind of departure from the church often follows months (or years) of asking serious questions. I'm always heartened to see church members asking good questions about what they believe. Far too many Christians through the ages have sought to maintain the engine of faith on the fumes of their father and mother's devotion, never wrestling with questions about not only *what* they believe but *why*. Far be it from me to chastise anyone else for pushing and prodding those areas of Christianity that cause them anxiety. Examining pressure points does not indicate one's faith is weak, but that *the* faith is strong—solid enough to withstand such inquiry.

Unfortunately, some go beyond wrestling with questions and doubts in order to better grasp and fully own their faith; they arrive at a "deconstruction" phase. Christianity no longer seems plausible. They reject teachings they once believed. Sometimes, they admit there are aspects of their faith journey they will miss, and so they wonder if a "newly revised" faith will permit them to maintain some semblance of what they had before. They are confident whatever Christianity they'd adopt after a period of deconstruction would be a better, more compelling version—a faith more "workable" for the times we live in. But for now, at least, they're not invested in revising the faith or seeking a new kind of Christianity at all; instead, they opt for fulfillment in other spiritual avenues that may offer purpose and meaning without requiring the affirmation of certain doctrines or adherence to a moral code.

Perhaps you're in a season of questioning, or have even arrived at a moment when "deconstruction" best describes your current state. I'd like to be upfront about three things in response.

First, whenever I address those who describe their faith journey in this way, I remain committed to doing my best to persuade them of the truth and beauty of Christianity, because I hold on to the hope that a reconstructed faith on the other side of this journey of doubt can be stronger and more vibrant than anything they've experienced so far.

Second, a reconstructed faith will require recovering Christian orthodoxy, not departing from it. Let me put it this way: recovering your faith will include recovering *the* faith, not altering Christian words like "love" and "grace" and "mercy" by filling them with meanings derived from contemporary culture.

Third, no matter how long friends remain in a state of disbelief in the gospel and disobedience to the Lord, I remain devoted to them and their wellbeing—and that's why I pray they'd be haunted by the

Jesus of the Gospels until they are mesmerized by his power and love, taken with his beauty, and yearn to once again belong to his people.

TWO CATEGORIES OF DOUBT

Many of the most common doubts and struggles seem to fall into two categories, with some overlap between them. The first set focuses on the *veracity* of Christian teaching: *Is Christianity true?* It's easy to find some of Christianity's truth claims implausible. Can we really believe that Jesus was born of a virgin, that the miracles we read about in the Old and New Testaments truly occurred, and that the enchanted world of the Bible is a better description of reality than the scientific world of natural laws we experience every day? So many Christian stories—and doctrines like the full deity and full humanity of Christ—seem out of touch, irrelevant, or farfetched.

The second set of doubts focuses on the *goodness* of Christian teaching: *Is Christianity good?* As people scan Christianity's record over the centuries and see the wreckage left by many who've done atrocious things in Jesus's name, they grow unsettled with religious certainty that could lead to more acts of violence and unjust discrimination. Can we really believe the church is a force for good in the world when so many tragedies can be traced back to its members? Some aspects of Christianity's moral vision, in particular the commands regarding sexuality and marriage, seem backward and unworkable—the Bible's moral aspirations unattainable.

At first when you encounter doubts, you may try to salvage a Christian identity that remains true to at least one of the sets. Perhaps you think you can hold on to the foundational truth claims of Christianity—the resurrection of Jesus, for instance, or other statements found in the Apostles' Creed—and still remake and revise the moral vision of Christianity so that it better corresponds to contemporary notions of goodness and freedom. Or maybe you think you can focus on a renewed moral vision that includes all the teachings of Christianity that resonate with you—loving your neighbor as yourself, showing grace to the outcast, the stranger, even your enemy—while downplaying or reinterpreting some of the miracle stories that feel embarrassing in an age of technological advance. Many people want to maintain *something* resembling Christianity, since they believe religions are good when they provide us with purpose and make us kinder and more decent to others. But such attempts to keep part of Christianity without the whole, or to revise it according to our preferences, only leaves us unsatisfied.

MY REASONS FOR HOPE

This brings us to what many describe as their deconstruction. Some in this state will say that they've not written off Christianity for good. Still, they believe it no longer accurate to describe themselves as Christian. Questions and doubts prohibit them from identifying with historic Christianity. Perhaps this is where you are as you read this chapter. While this news always saddens me, I have hope that your Christian faith can be recovered. Here's why.

First, I admire anyone who has the integrity to give up the fruitless pursuit of molding and changing the Christian faith into an identity that better suits them, no matter how distant it may be from orthodoxy. Using the language of deconstruction rightly acknowledges that whatever spirituality someone may still claim, it's not historic Christianity. To claim a Christian identity while holding non-Christian beliefs would be intellectually dishonest—both for you and for other Christians.

Second, I'm heartened by anyone who has tenacity in asking questions and searching for answers. What's more, even though you realize that this deconversion has cost you friendships and relationships, you seem committed to following the truth wherever it may lead. In some church contexts, it would be far easier to suppress questions and shut down doubts than to risk the crisis of identity that comes from wrestling with deep matters of faith.

Third, if you describe yourself as deconstructed and yet remain committed to asking questions, I have hope that in your continual pursuit of truth the Holy Spirit will bring clarity and illumination to you. If not for the Holy Spirit, there would be no hope of *anyone* continuing in the faith, myself included, so I don't place my hopes for your recovery of Christianity in yourself, your questions, or (certainly not!) my answers, but in the Spirit whose work is essential in opening eyes and hearts to the beauty of Jesus and the love of his people.

ASK MORE QUESTIONS

How, though, should I respond to deconversion, to the doubts and questions that have now overwhelmed someone's Christian identity? You might expect me to tell you simply to "have faith," to set aside these doubts and take a leap: believe something to be true before you're convinced of its veracity or goodness. But this response makes the Christian faith seem too disconnected from tough questions.

No, the last thing I'd want you to do is to suppress your questions and squelch your doubts. Instead, I hope you'll discover *more* questions and entertain *more* doubts. You heard me right. You need to doubt more. You need to question more.

To be fair in your pursuit of truth, you should take those doubts and questions that you, with laser-like focus, have trained on Christianity and point them at the story you've adopted for yourself. Until now, your faith in yourself and in deconstruction has escaped the level of intense scrutiny that you put your earlier Christian faith through. If you truly deconstruct in a way that is authentic and honest, then your newfound faith must undergo the same level of examination as your older faith.

Here's what I mean. Let's start with the first set of doubts you may have entertained—those that concern the *truthfulness* of Christianity. Apply them to yourself. What reasons do you have for believing that your doubts come from a neutral and honest heart? What if you are not the dispassionate pursuer of "facts" you perceive yourself to be, but are instead shaped by assumptions and presuppositions you've never challenged? Do you believe all religious claims to truth are relative? If so, why? What evidence do you have for seeing the world only in natural terms? How does your current cultural environment make this way of life seem plausible to you? Is it possible you've merely traded one set of unproven assumptions for another?

In the same way, scrutinize your questions about the *goodness* of Christianity. Who determines goodness? Where do you get that sense of goodness? Could it be that the measures by which you judge the inadequacies of the church are the standards the church has bequeathed to you? Take those doubts you have about Christianity and point them back to your own heart. What if the questions you have about the goodness of Christianity are rooted in a desire to justify yourself, to showcase your goodness, to change places with God so that you're the one with the gavel?

Perhaps you're puzzled by my description of your "newfound faith." You may have grown so accustomed to thinking in terms of deconstruction that you'd rather say that you now have no faith at all, or that you are spiritual in a broad and vague sense instead of in a particular way. But I don't believe you are faithless. Your faith has merely shifted—away from God and his Word and toward yourself and the story you've crafted, in which you now find meaning and significance. Your sense of belonging has shifted also—away from the people of God who confess faith in and allegiance to Jesus, and toward people who affirm your deconversion. You've been conditioned by your cultural context and your new community to see doubt as courageous. Instead of finding your identity and purpose within the story of the Bible, you have adopted a faith that follows the contours of the Enlightenment's story of the world: *There once was a time when you believed in superstition and religious dogma, but now you've dared to strike out on your own, reject the faith of the dark ages of your past, free yourself from your church, and become the hero who makes your own way in life.*

Make no mistake: you're still on a faith journey; it's just that the way you tell your story has changed. Will *that* story receive as much scrutiny as the Christian story you've rejected? Will your new community be held to the same standards as your old community? Will your *self* receive as much critical examination as your Savior did?

Until thinkers ask more questions of their deconstruction, I believe they are trading faiths—merely accepting (on faith) a new story that gives meaning and significance to their life. They've not yet put their new assumptions under the microscope. For example, why do people accept the idea that it's broad-minded to reject miracles in favor of a naturalistic view of the world, when the *Christian* mind is broad enough to believe in both natural laws and supernatural intervention? Or why do some believe it right to reject certain aspects of Christianity's moral teaching when the basis for their rejection relies on other aspects of Christianity's moral vision—a worldview that has so permeated our societal norms and expectations that we don't even notice it?

Remember, there is always more going on in our hearts and minds than we understand. Christianity can withstand rigorous examination of its truth and goodness. The question is: can your newfound faith, as expressed in your deconversion story, withstand the same level of interrogation? You are no longer sure about the *God* of Christianity; are you sure of the *self* you place at the center of your deconversion story?

RETAINING AN OPEN MIND

As you submit your story and your new beliefs to new sets of questions, I hope you'll keep an open mind toward the teachings of Christianity you once adhered to. If you do, I believe you'll find you resonate more with the fundamental tenets of Christianity than you might expect. So many deconstruction stories replace the cosmic drama of good and evil—with the cross and resurrection of Christ at the center of a number of life-giving, marvelous paradoxes—with the individual quest to self-discovery. The pursuit of the self, however, leads to an emptier and shallower life, a road toward nothingness—something far removed from the blessed vision described by Christianity and a true union with God that overwhelms yet never obliterates our unique personalities. Over and over again, doctrines that may seem distasteful or implausible in our day may surprise you.

Take, for example, the idea that all human beings are marked by sinfulness—that we are not basically good but basically evil. That's hard to swallow by many today who find it more dignifying to think of humanity as basically good, with the propensity for corruption and mistakes. But what if *this* doctrine, as difficult as it may sound, proves to be a great equalizing force that puts the prince at the same moral level as the pauper, and issues the call of repentance to all people regardless of rank or status or prestige? Another example: the belief that a good God created the world and made humans in his image, so that all of us have dignity and value and bear moral responsibility. That idea makes little sense to a world in which matter is all there is, or a society in which people scoff at the idea that a divine Judge would hold us accountable for our actions. But what if this doctrine, challenging as it may be, provides the basis for believing in human rights and treating others with dignity, while the secular view must admit that commitment to "human rights" is grounded in nothing more than a useful fiction that helps society to function?

RECOVERING ORTHODOXY

It's not surprising that, in a secular age, people wrestle with doubts and questions. We are always tempted to challenge the constraints of orthodoxy at the pressure points where we most *need* the constraints of orthodoxy. In every culture and in every age, parts of Christianity seem implausible. Aspects of orthodoxy seem strange. *Truth* is strange. We didn't invent it. Fiction makes more sense. Heresy always seems reasonable. Deconstruction appeals to us because it launches a new faith that better suits the story we want to tell about ourselves.

Christianity, however, is more alive than we are. This faith refuses to embrace our error, no matter how sincerely held, and insists instead on keeping us from error, by believing in the ultimate triumph of truth. Deconstruction binds us to the movement of the current moment; Christianity frees us from slavery to the present day.

That's why I encourage you to do what is truly "provocative" and "daring"—not to ask more questions of Christianity or your former church, but to turn those questions upon yourself. In an age when people believe they can pick and choose which parts of any religion to adhere to, it's truly astounding when someone submits to truth beyond themselves and their changing intuitions.

DIFFERENT STORY

That's why, if you are in a state of deconstruction, I hope you'll reconsider Christianity as you commit to asking more questions. You've interrogated your faith; now is the time to interrogate yourself. And as you do so, remember this: the Jesus whose words and actions changed the world—who leaps from the pages of the Gospels into our hearts and minds, the incomparable figure who bursts out of any box we'd put him in and breaks the chains of every cultural expectation—this

Jesus loves doubters. He told Thomas he is the Way, the Truth, and the Life, but when Thomas couldn't and wouldn't believe, Jesus gave him a close-up of his scars of love.

Jesus is alive. He continues to surprise people today, and I pray he'll surprise you. And I hope that one day, maybe soon, you'll look back and see how God used this season of deconversion in a manner similar to the way a broken limb can actually wind up stronger and more fortified at the very place the break occurred. Broken limbs, deconstruction stories—neither of these is good, but Jesus is all about bringing good things from bad. He can resurrect life from the grave of a buried faith. I can't wait to read the next chapter in your story.

2

'PROGRESSIVE' CHRISTIANITY WAS EVEN SHALLOWER THAN THE EVANGELICAL FAITH I LEFT

IAN HARBER

In John 6, Jesus's hard teaching causes a large number of his followers to abandon him. After they leave, Jesus asks his remaining disciples, "Do you want to go away as well?" (v. 67). Peter, whom I assume is heartbroken and embarrassed from seeing so many he knows leave the one he calls Lord, speaks up: "Lord, to whom shall we go? You have the words of eternal life, and we have believed, and have come to know, that you are the Holy One of God" (vv. 68–69).

This story is my story. I have walked in both shoes: the shoes of those who deserted and the shoes of Peter who couldn't leave, no matter how hard it seemed to stay. I was an #exvangelical who left the faith of my youth for "progressive Christianity." Then I returned. Here's my #revangelical story.

HOW MY FAITH CRUMBLED

The Christian tradition I grew up in—for all the wonderful things it gave me—was not prepared for a generation of kids with access to high-speed internet. Not that the critiques of the Bible we discovered online were new, but they were now at the fingertips of curious folks who grew up in evangelical bubbles. Like me. The answers given in church seemed shallow compared to the legitimate critiques that were a Google search or YouTube video away. *What about the contradictions and scientific inaccuracies in certain biblical stories? How have we ever shrugged at the passages in which God commands Israel to slaughter her enemies and their children? How could a loving God condemn his beloved creation to eternal torment? What about all the other religions? Aren't they all saying basically the same thing?* These questions, among others, began to chip away at the authority of the stories I was handed as a child.

Not only did I have questions about the Bible, but I had questions about how it squared with my faith's political culture. *Why did our policies seem to particularly disadvantage poor and marginalized communities? Why was it common in the church to see Christians degrade immigrants, made in the image of God, who were simply seeking a better life in my Texas town? As important as abortion is, surely we're supposed to care about those suffering* after *birth as well, right?*

I couldn't help but think it had to be more complicated than the story I was being told.

So eventually, I left the faith completely. I wanted nothing to do with Jesus or the church.

Interestingly, it was in a time of mourning—when I learned that my mother, from whom I had been estranged, had died at 33 (I was

16)—that God began to reenter my life. But my evangelical environment lacked a substantial theology of suffering. Suffering was something to avoid or suppress, not a means of God's transforming grace in our lives.

This triangle of questions—about Scripture, politics, and suffering—laid the foundation for me to explore progressive Christianity.

DECONSTRUCTION WITHOUT RECONSTRUCTION

I read Rob Bell's books *Velvet Elvis* and *Love Wins*. I read Donald Miller's *Blue Like Jazz*. I still remember the paragraph from *Blue Like Jazz* that opened me up to a world of grace I hadn't experienced—but also to a world freed from orthodox doctrine. As a fan of Michael Gungor, I began listening to his newly launched podcast, The Liturgists.

The views I encountered were thrilling. Science did not have to be discarded because of the Bible! When prayer felt like a coin toss, mysticism provided a new way to encounter the divine! Faith could inspire politics that included care for marginalized groups! Most important, in hearing Michael Gungor and "Science Mike" McHargue's stories of deconstruction, I heard my story. I found people who understood what it was like to deconstruct your faith and have to rebuild it from scratch.

But then I ran into a problem. As I kept listening and reading, I realized I didn't have the tools to rebuild—and I wasn't receiving any from these voices. Every belief I held had been neatly disassembled and laid bare on the floor for examination. But there was no guidance for putting something back together. Helping people deconstruct their faith without also helping put it back together again is lazy, irresponsible, dangerous, and isolating. The goal of deconstruction should be greater faithfulness to Jesus, not mere self-discovery or signaling one's virtue.

As The Liturgists' journeys progressed, they fell in increasing lockstep with the progressive platform of the political Left. It reminded me of the conformity of conservative Christians to whatever the Republican Party told them to believe. When the 2016 election ended, I had a strange experience. I shared the progressives' concern for the country, but I also saw them using the same litmus tests that the conservative evangelicals of my youth had used—just now on the other side of the aisle. Now, if you held to a historic Christian sexual ethic, you were a backward bigot. If you considered abortion morally wrong, you were anti-woman.

Progressives had become just as fundamentalist as the fundamentalists they despised. Only now, instead of the litmus test being traditional values, it was wokeness. If you didn't tow the party line of progressive orthodoxy, you were an outcast. A heretic.

'PROGRESSIVE' BRAND. SAME OLD SUPERFICIAL PITCH.

I'd heard about the dangers of moralistic therapeutic deism (MTD), the default American religion in which God simply wants you to live a decent life, not be sad, and he doesn't intrude on your life. I originally ran to progressive Christianity to counter that kind of shallow belief. But what I found was more of the same, only with new definitions.

 Wokeness was the new morality. Therapy was the new path to happiness. Cancel culture was the new church discipline. And like MTD, there was, conveniently, no personal God to place demands on your life in any meaningful way. In this "progressive" MTD, Elizabeth Gilbert's trope is the only thing left: "God dwells within you, as you." There's no way to distinguish between ourselves and God. In this paradigm, we *are* God.

I'm not anti-woke or anti-therapy. Systemic injustice is real, and we need some of the conversations that wokeness has brought us. I was in therapy for almost two years while in college, and I think it can benefit many of us. But in the end, these do not replace the eternal love of the triune God.

Mark Sayers describes the progressive vision of the world as "the kingdom without the King." We want all of God's blessings—without submitting to his loving rule and reign. We want progress—without his presence. We want justice—without his justification. We want the horizontal implications of the gospel for society—without the vertical reconciliation of sinners with God. We want society to conform to our standard of moral purity—without God's standard of personal holiness.

JOURNEY BACK TO ORTHODOX FAITH

After the 2016 election I became convinced it was time to begin re-building my faith. A few months later, two things happened simulta-neously: I began formal theological education and, in a tragic accident, I lost the grandfather who had raised me. This death plunged me into another season of intense suffering, but this time in a theologically rigorous environment.

One of my teachers said, "We do theology in the light so we can stand on it in the dark." I was doing theology *and* standing on it in the dark. For the first time I really learned the doctrines of the Trinity and of Scripture as a unified story, and how to read it as inspired literature. I was taught how doctrines that I assumed were contradictory—like penal substitution and Christus Victor—actually need each other to form the full, beautiful, biblical picture. I learned about union with Christ and all the blessings it brings. I learned about spiritual disci-plines and the life-giving freedom that flows from a disciplined pur-suit of God. From there, the wide and rich world of historic Christian orthodoxy swung open for me to explore.

We need *more* theology, nuance, grace, compassion, and under-standing in our churches, not less. But these things are made possible *by* orthodox doctrine, not in spite of it. Doubt and questions need not catalyze a pendulum swing from belief to unbelief. If worked out in a healthy, thoughtful Christian community—and with an abiding con-nection to Christ, our true vine (John 15)—they can actually deepen faith and strengthen roots, producing a life where we bear fruit and withstand the fierce winds of a secular age.

If you're reading this, there's a chance you have begun the process of deconstruction in one way or another. Maybe it's questions about science or confusion around suffering. Maybe it's a slew of difficult passages in the Bible that don't square with your picture of God. May-be it's frustration with the political status quo. But for one reason or another, you're pulling apart the building blocks of a faith you once took for granted but now wonder if there's any truth to. If that is where you are today, I understand. And as you begin this journey of reexamining your faith, there are three things I would like you to hear.

First, I'm grieved there are not more places where you can feel safe with your doubts and questions. Your doubts and questions deserve to be searched out and taken seriously. Too many churches have dismissed reasonable questions as a slippery slope to atheism. I cannot promise that your questions will be met with grace and good faith where you are, and that saddens me.

However, don't let one church experience—or even two or three—represent the totality of all churches. Even if it seems the people around you cannot hold the weight of your doubts and questions, plenty of churches out there *will* treat you, and your doubts, with the intellectual patience and respect you deserve. Moreover, saints throughout church history can help. And even more so, God can. Don't give up on the faith because one church gave up on you.

Second, you might be thinking I want you to stop deconstructing—to turn around and stay exactly where you are—but that would be wrong. Keep going. Parts of your faith probably *do* need to be deconstructed. Your legitimate questions *do* need to be addressed. These need not be steps away from faith, but steps toward a deeper and lasting faith. Don't stuff these questions down and hope they go away. Don't settle for less than the good, true, and beautiful found in Jesus Christ.

In your deconstruction, you will likely encounter teachings about God that you haven't heard before, that resonate in a way you haven't felt before, and that promise an "Ultimate Reality" freed from the pages of an ancient book. And while that promise sounds nice, I can tell you firsthand that it only leads to more confusion, exhaustion, and inconsistencies.

I'd contend that your problem isn't with God or Jesus or even the Bible; it's that no one has showed you the riches contained in Christ and mined through a careful study of Scripture. A teacher never went into the storeroom and brought out treasures old and new. Instead, you were handed a "believe it or leave it" theology that left little room for growth and grace.

There is more to Christ than meets the eye. He's like a treasure hidden in a field (Matt. 13:44–46). A man found the treasure and sold everything he had to buy the field, just so he could have the treasure.

You're going to have to dig, and perhaps sell what you have, to reach the treasure. But the treasure is so precious, it's worth it.

Third, as you deconstruct, you'll likely encounter the world of mysticism. You'll be told that God is a vague mystery, not something we can truly know. You'll hear that, instead of trying to have all the right answers like those staunch fundamentalists, you should embrace the mystery and strive to touch the divine.

Don't buy that false dichotomy. There is more than enough room in the historic Christian tradition and biblical witness for the mystery of God. In this life, we see through a glass dimly (1 Cor. 13:12). We'll never have all the answers. There are things we will get wrong. And yet God will still love us even as we miss the mark.

But don't let this truth blind you to another glorious truth: that this mysterious, transcendent God has made himself known. His heart has always been—from the first page of the Bible to the last—to dwell with his people in never-ending joy. While God is high and above all things, he's also intimately involved in our lives and our world. And while you'll never know everything or find answers to every single question, you can still know him. Not in an impersonal "God is in all things so just be aware of him" kind of way. But as a friend, comforter, coworker, shepherd, and even Father. Yes, God is a mystery. But he can also be known. He is known in Jesus. He is known in the pages of Scripture. And when we seek him with all of our heart, we will find him.

Everyone's faith journey is winding and complex. But God is God, and he lays out a path so we can find him, even when we've wandered from what's familiar. There are more paths than ever before in today's world—more options for spiritual "enlightenment" or custom faith. But no path leads to true happiness and everlasting life except "Jesus alone" (John 14:6), which is narrower than we might like (Matt. 7:13) but more satisfying than we can imagine (Ps. 16:11).

In my journey I discovered, with Peter, that God's "divine power has granted to us all things that pertain to life and godliness, through the knowledge of him who called us to his own glory and excellence" (2 Pet. 1:3). In Christ, we have everything we need. Why leave the boundaries of faith "once for all delivered to the saints" (Jude 1:3) in order to find life? Jesus has the words of life. He *is* life, the truth, and the way. Where else would we go?

3

DECONVERSION IS NOT AS COUNTERCULTURAL AS YOU THINK

BRETT MCCRACKEN

In recent years, the "Instagram deconversion announcement" has become a well-established genre. The formula is pronounced: a former evangelical author, pastor, CCM star, or simply "raised in the church" 20-something posts a self-portrait looking ponderous and solemn, yet free. Maybe they're seen from behind, looking out at some beautiful lake or mountain scene. Perhaps they carefully select a "this is me, warts and all" selfie with perfectly imperfect styling. The post's accompanying text usually begins with some variation of "I never thought I would say this" or "It's terrifying to post this," followed by a lengthy narrative involving some combination of words such as "evolving," "journey," "fear," "discovery," "honesty," "authentic," "free," and "hopeful."

I don't mean to diminish the sincere agonizing and legitimate trepidation that accompanies an individual's decision to make a de-conversion "Instagram official." I'm just observing that this has become a genre—a predictable, commonplace, and not-at-all surprising artifact of a "find yourself" age.

Far from renegade, edgy, and brave, the announcement of a person's conscious uncoupling from institutional religion is simply going with the flow of a culture that mainstreamed such behavior decades ago. Rather than going against the grain of Western culture, abandoning received doctrine and institutional faith—in favor of a self-styled, follow-your-heart spirituality—is quite smoothly "with the grain." To declare one's spiritual autonomy, one's unshackling from Christianity's "constraints" and old-fashioned ideas about sin and morality, is simply to nod along with Oprah and her vast tribe of suburban moms. To disown a God of limitations, boundaries, and wrath—in favor of a God who only wants to fund your "best life" dreams and promote John Lennon–style "love" and good vibes—is to join the ranks of frat boys obsessed with Joe Rogan, "name it and claim it" prosperity preachers, and the vast majority of bestselling authors in "religion, spirituality, and faith" of the last 20 years.

So before you file divorce papers from the Christianity of your youth, know that doing so is in no way countercultural. Like marital divorce, it's thoroughly acceptable and common. I want to suggest that the far more radical—and truly countercultural—choice isn't to abandon Christian faith because it is maddening, difficult, and out of step with the contemporary zeitgeist.

The radical choice is to keep the faith.

HAVE YOU GIVEN TRUE CHRISTIANITY A TRY?

When I say keeping the faith is radical, I'm talking about Christian faith in the true, biblical sense. I'm not talking about an American cultural Christianity in which doctrinal literacy is low but concern for gun rights and a border wall is high. Nor am I talking about a progressive Christianity that selectively invokes Scripture for justice campaigns but ignores its personal moral demands. "Deconstructing" comfortable forms of Christianity is good. To keep the faith of these distorted forms of Christianity is in no way radical.

But I would encourage you, if you're considering a break from Christianity, to make sure you've given real Christianity a try. This Christianity doesn't fit neatly with your politics and preferences but constantly presses you on different fronts, refusing to be boxed in or manipulated into what you want it to be. This Christianity doesn't simply affirm you as you are but relentlessly pushes you to become more like Jesus.

This Christianity invites—rather than shuns—the intellectual wrestling that naturally comes when we try to wrap our minds around an infinite, triune God whose existence and work in the world will always be a bit mysterious. Many who deconstruct their faith believe Christianity is a religion for intellectual simpletons, in which everything is explainable and all tensions must be resolved (out of fear that they'll discredit the whole thing). If that's your experience of Christianity, I'm sorry. I understand why you'd want to leave it behind. But that's not true Christianity; it's simply another mutation of the faith—an attempt to domesticate God and shoehorn him into our comfortable paradigms. True Christianity always challenges our paradigms and assaults our comfort. It's rewarding for sure, but also costly.

One of its costs is intellectual—the taxing burden of lingering questions, knotty paradoxes, and "mirror dimly" faith (1 Cor. 13:12) without empirical proof. But that's what true faith is. It requires a humble willingness to be content with not comprehending everything. The late theologian J. I. Packer once expressed it this way:

> It is not for us to stop believing because we lack understanding, or to postpone believing till we can get understanding, but to believe in order that we may understand; as Augustine said, "unless you believe, you will not understand." Faith first, sight afterwards, is God's order, not *vice versa*; and the proof of the sincerity of our faith is our willingness to have it so.[1]

---

1.   J. I. Packer, *"Fundamentalism" and the Word of God* (Grand Rapids, MI: Eerdmans, 1958), 109.

If this is what Christian faith actually requires—a willingness to have "faith first, sight afterwards"—then I'd suggest that to keep believing in this faith is a braver and costlier choice than abandoning it because you can't fully wrap your mind around its thornier components.

BOURGEOIS COMFORT (AND LONELINESS) OF BESPOKE SPIRITUALITY

Chances are, if you're considering deconstructing institutional religion, you're not moving immediately to full-on atheism. Instead, you're likely planning to forge a more *intuitional*, bespoke spirituality that perhaps retains some aspects of Christianity but is more fluid, incorporating bits and pieces of other philosophies, rituals, and spiritualities as they fit your mood and needs. This is what religion columnist Tara Isabella Burton chronicles in *Strange Rites: New Religions for a Godless World*:

> A religion of emotive intuition, of aestheticized and commodified experience, of self-creation and self-improvement and, yes, selfies. . . . A religion decoupled from institutions, creeds, from metaphysical truth-claims about God or the universe or the Way Things Are, but that still seeks—in various and varying ways—to provide us with the pillars of what religion always has: meaning, purpose, community, ritual.[2]

This "mix and match" religion might include a few parts of traditional religion (Shabbat, Christmas carols, Catholic prayer candles), a smattering of "wellness" practices (yoga, meditation, SoulCycle), a dash of New Age magic (burning sage, Tarot cards, astrology), and a deeply moral zealotry for social justice or LGBT+ rights.

While this sort of remixed, bespoke spirituality might sound radical, in reality it's simply a bourgeois iteration of mainstream consumerism. Capitalism loves it, because it means more products and experiences to sell to ever-hungrier consumers looking for meaning outside the walls of religious institutions. But far from a countercul-

---

2.   Tara Isabella Burton, *Strange Rites: New Religions for a Godless World* (New York: Hachette, 2020), 2–3.

tural protest, to choose this sort of build-your-own religion is simply to fall in line with the "have it your way" Burger King brand of faith. In our intensely consumeristic world, the person who resists the urge to curate a bespoke spirituality—and instead sticks with a consistent, established religious tradition even when it doesn't fit personal preferences—is the true radical.

It's also worth noting that bespoke spirituality is something typically only chosen by the privileged—those with the comfort, means, and social status suitable for an (often quite expensive) adventure in à la carte spirituality. The privileged can detach from institutions and meander on their intuitional paths with little concern for the possible dangers of a "go it alone" spirituality. Less privileged people recognize the necessity—not just for survival, but for flourishing—of embeddedness within social fabrics, institutions, and traditions. It's perhaps not surprising that atheism and agnosticism are uncommon among lower-income classes and in developing nations. You have to live a pretty comfortable life to be a religious "none."

To ditch religion in favor of bespoke spirituality (or no spirituality) is thus a bourgeois choice fully in keeping with comfortable consumerism. Not only does it not make you a renegade, but it also makes you lonely. Because when you depart Christianity, you aren't opening yourself up to a new, more spacious freedom. Quite the opposite. You're narrowing your freedom and horizons of possibility to the confines of one person: you. While it sounds great—and again, is totally the way of our consumerist iWorld—this me-driven spirituality eventually becomes claustrophobic and lonely. By freeing yourself from the constraints of community, the demands of external authority, and the accountability of institutional formation, it may seem at first like you're choosing an open-road, idyllic freedom. But freedom isn't the absence of constraints. Jesus didn't say "total, limitless autonomy will set you free." He said the truth will set you free (John 8:32). Not *your* truth; *the* truth, in a true-for-everyone sense. And that sort of freeing truth isn't easily found by looking within, trusting your gut, and going it alone.

RADICAL COST OF TRUE CHRISTIANITY

In a post-Christian and rapidly secularizing culture, deconstructing isn't a radical act. It's just a normal thing that more and more people do. And it makes sense! Historic Christianity is an ever stranger, ever more fringe, ever more unwelcome thing in today's world. Consider all the ways it subverts current norms in Western culture:

- In a "believe in yourself" world, Christianity calls you to deny yourself (Matt. 16:24) and take up your cross (Luke 14:27).
- In a "you do you" world that emphasizes expressive individualism, authenticity, and nonconformity, Christianity is about conforming to the likeness of Jesus (Rom. 8:29) and being imitators of God (Eph. 5:1).
- In a consumerist and greedy culture, Christianity calls you to costly generosity (Luke 21:1–4) and a willingness to give up material possessions (Matt. 19:21; Luke 14:33).
- In a self-oriented world of self-promotion, self-help, and selfies, Christianity calls you to be an others-focused servant (Phil. 2:3–4; Gal. 6:2; Matt. 20:26–28).
- In a world that says you should be free to do with your body whatever you wish, Christianity says you ought to glorify God with your body (1 Cor. 6:20).
- In a sexually progressive culture that sanctions pretty much anything in the bedroom, as long as it's consensual, Christianity says sex is intended for the covenantal union of one man and one woman (Gen. 2:24; Matt. 19:3–6; 1 Cor. 7:2).
- In a world that privileges power, "winning," and "best life" success, Christianity calls you to value weakness (2 Cor. 12:9–10).
- In a partisan world in which thinking the worst of your enemies and trying to "own" them on social media is a way of life, Christianity calls you to the radical challenge of loving them (Matt. 5:44).
- In a world that has normalized the discarding of unborn lives and the dehumanizing of others through racism, sexism, and xenophobia, Christianity insists all humans bear the image of God (Gen. 1:27) and are worthy of dignity and protection.

- In a world fraught with division and tribal fragmentation, in which it's easier than ever before to part ways with someone who differs from you, Christianity calls you to be reconciled (Eph. 2:11–22).
- In a pluralistic world with a diversity of beliefs—in which "all roads lead to heaven" is a comforting thought—Christianity calls you to believe there is only one path to heaven: trusting in Jesus Christ (John 14:6).
- In a world steeped in scientific rationalism, Christianity requires belief in the supernatural (a virgin conceiving a child, bodies resurrecting from the dead, people being miraculously healed, among many other examples).

None of this is easy to practice or believe. And the list could be much longer. There's nothing comfortable about truly following Jesus. Those who say otherwise—or whose version of Christianity is conveniently custom-fit to their personal comfort (whether politics, music preferences, or sexual proclivities)—are deceiving themselves and harming the cause of Christ.

The reality is, to accept all the costs of true Christianity, to believe all it asserts, to go against the grain of the culture so dramatically—is incredibly difficult and a little weird. If Christians are labeled "freaks" for what they believe and practice in today's world, it's for good reason. We should not be surprised that few follow this narrow path (Matt. 7:13–14). We shouldn't be shocked that deconversion announcements on Instagram are common.

Do you really want to be countercultural? Then don't abandon Christianity. Stick with it.

4

DON'T DECONSTRUCT— DISENCULTURATE INSTEAD

HUNTER BEAUMONT

What if Christianity isn't synonymous with your childhood church? What if you could return to faith, and discover the actual Jesus, but it wouldn't be like going back to what you left?

In my years as a pastor, I've asked many people these questions. The stories that prompt them have a common arc: "I grew up inside the church, but now I've reached a point that my faith isn't satisfying." Usually this statement concurs with significant life shifts—leaving home, going to college, dating, marrying, not marrying, moving to our sunny and progressive city. Most of my interlocutors have questions or concerns that their "Christian upbringing" hardly seems to care about. They also have new friends who lead fulfilling lives without religion. A Sunday morning of Eggs Benedict, Bloody Marys, and brunch conversation is a more invigorating liturgy than songs and sermons.

If you've faced this dilemma, you might assume there are only two choices: suppress your misgivings and keep trudging along, or deconstruct your faith by doubting the whole enterprise. I want to help you break free from this binary.

DISENCULTURATED GOSPEL

Is there really a way to return to Christianity without going back to what you left? Might it even result in a thicker faith?

Yes!

We can learn a lesson, actually, from missionaries. They translate the gospel of Jesus from one culture to another. Like a kernel protected by an outer husk, the gospel (kernel) is always encased in a culture (husk). The missionary's job is to ensure that the gospel kernel is free to enter new cultures without being captive to its old husk. This process is called "disenculturation," and it can help you discover a faith that contains all the riches of original Christianity without the dry husk of your old religious subculture.[1]

I experienced this long before learning the word "disenculturation." When I was in high school, my family moved to a new city and my parents enrolled me in a private school. They wanted to prepare me for college, and the school had a reputation for academic rigor. It was also a "Christian school," founded by a big evangelical church. Up until this point, I had never been inside anything called evangelical. We were mainline Methodists of a liberal bent. All I knew of evangelicals was that a Baptist youth group had once tried to trick me

---

1.   For an in-depth discussion see "Secondary Elements of Renewal" in Richard Lovelace, *Dynamics of Spiritual Life: An Evangelical Theology of Renewal*, expanded ed. (Downers Grove, IL: IVP Academic, 2020), 145–200, and "Translation in Mission" in Darrell L. Guder, *The Continuing Conversion of the Church*, Gospel and Our Culture (Grand Rapids, MI: Wm. B. Eerdmans, 2000), 73–96.

into "getting saved" by offering pizza and access to the cool crowd. I recognized the trap and kept my distance.

Inside this school, I could no longer keep my distance. And to my surprise, I didn't mind these evangelicals. Their faith was living and active. In my Methodist churches, we turned up every week, said the creed, listened to a boring sermon by a preacher who didn't sound like he believed the creed, and went home without giving it a second thought. These evangelicals, on the other hand, studied their faith and lived it out.

They were also meticulously clear on what they called "the gospel." Under their teaching, I learned its tenets, and I was surprised to find that God does not justify "good people" but rather sinful people who trust Jesus. *This is not Christianity*, I thought, but the teachers patiently showed it to me in the Bible. Accepting all of this seemed to awaken something new inside me.

There were other aspects of this evangelical world that I found amusing and unconvincing. They had their own pop music, and it wasn't as good as real pop music. There was a pantheon of B-list celebrities. Some evangelical athlete or musician or preacher or strongman who tore phone books in half often came to perform at our chapel service. They were in love with Republicans. Their college fair was full of non–Southeastern Conference schools like Wheaton College and Gordon College that I had never heard of. My girlfriend was not allowed to watch PG-13 movies even though we were 17. Then there were the creepy talks on the dangers of sex and STDs, part of a tendency to teach "Christian values" using fear.

Still perceiving everything through the eyes of an outsider, I kept my concerns to myself. I loved the gospel even though the other stuff was weird, so I sorted this new world into a "keep" bucket and an "ignore" bucket. But I also noticed that for most evangelicals there were no buckets. It was a one-package deal, presented as "authentic Christianity."

In the years after high school, many of my friends who had been raised in that world started to question or walk away from the faith. There were two common themes.

First, they experienced the reverse culture shock leaving the evangelical bubble that I had experienced moving into it. Having lived their whole lives inside it, they had heard of the outside world through caricatures but had scant personal knowledge of it. When they finally left the bubble, they met good, interesting people who didn't share their faith. They discovered that life outside is fun, not the gloom and doom they'd been trained to expect. They developed new questions, but their evangelical churches offered only simple answers. In fact, the gospel had been taught in such thin terms that they didn't realize it was deeper, able to handle hard questions.

Second, they had no way to differentiate what parts to keep and what to let go. For example, they didn't know they had permission to retain the gospel while rethinking their politics. Nor could they see the difference between the Christian sex ethic and the guilt trips used to teach it to teenagers. It was all one package, and to doubt any part of the package was to doubt the whole thing.

I wished I could give them my buckets.

A decade later I was in graduate school, taking a class on missions. I learned that missionaries take the gospel from one culture to another. To do this well, they have to differentiate it from their sending culture. This process enables them to give people the gospel without also handing them a bucketful of white elephants. Certain cultural artifacts can be confusing and even offensive, a barrier to the gospel for people in another culture. *My friends need the same thing!* I thought. Evangelical subculture had become a barrier to the gospel. They needed a disenculturated faith just as much as an unreached people group did.

DISENCULTURATION IN SCRIPTURE

As it turns out, disenculturation isn't just helpful, it's biblical—a healthy habit of vital Christianity. The gospel breaking out from Jewish culture is one of the central plotlines in Acts. When a culturally versatile church emerged in Antioch, the Spirit used two Jewish leaders from this church to ignite mission to the Gentiles (Acts 11–14). Paul and Barnabas led many Gentiles to faith and trained them to follow Jesus *in* their culture. Many other Jewish believers were confused, since they assumed anyone who shared their gospel would also convert to their culture and obey all the old covenant's dietary and ceremonial laws. But at the Jerusalem Council, God led the apostles and elders to differentiate essential gospel from Jewish customs (Acts 15).[2]

The growth of the Jesus movement thereafter shows the gospel's power when freed from its husk. In one of his letters, Paul describes the cultural flexibility that fueled his mission:

> To the Jews, I became as a Jew, in order to win Jews. To those under the law I became as one under the law (though not myself under the law) that I might win those under the law. To those outside the law I became as one outside the law (not being outside the law of God but under the law of Christ) that I might win those outside the law. To the weak I became weak, that I might win the weak. I have become all things to all people, that by all means I might save some. I do it all for the sake of the gospel, that I may share with them its blessings. (1 Cor. 9:20–23)

From Paul's other writings, we know he saw the gospel as a message of reconciliation to God through repentance and faith in Jesus. He insisted no other requirements be added to this message. Such clarity on what is and isn't gospel allowed him to take up the habits of various cultures, so long as the gospel was kept distinct. We can summarize Paul's mindset like this: "It's possible to believe the gospel but not live according to the Jewish culture in which I was raised. My gospel can be lived out in *many different* cultures."

So cling closely to the gospel but hold loosely to religious subculture. You're on solid, biblical ground to do so. It might not be easy. Paul was under constant pressure to re-enculturate to Judaism. But it could reinvigorate your faith.

2. In the chapter "Secondary Elements of Renewal" in *Dynamics of Spiritual Life*, Lovelace has a rich analysis of disenculturation in the early Jesus movement beginning with Antioch and continuing through Paul's ministry.

HOW TO START

Here are some ideas for getting started on this journey.

1. LEARN TO SEE CULTURE

Like a fish in water who doesn't feel wet, we often don't recognize our culture, the languages and stories that explain our world. Cultures foster habits that compose the good life and defense mechanisms that deflect the questions of outsiders. They elevate celebrities who exemplify their ideals. Then, having done all this, cultures pull a sneaky move: they pretend they don't exist. They present themselves as "just the way things are." But culture is always present, and it always plays a role in our experience of faith.

This means that the first step is to learn to see culture and its power. My friends who grew up inside the evangelical subculture didn't start doubting Christianity until they had left it. Coincidence? Probably not. The subculture had propped up their faith.

But this also means that culture contributed to their newfound questions. What many call "doubt" is actually a culture shift that displaces the old plausibility structures. What many call "deconstructing my faith" is actually a change of cultural locations that causes me to rethink old assumptions. When you learn to see the power of culture, you see what's really happening: You learned Christianity in one culture. Now you've moved to a new culture. The first step, then, is to recognize this for what it is—tension caused by a culture shift and not necessarily by Christianity.[3]

---

3.   It's also possible to experience a culture shift without moving from one place to another, given the rise of mass media and connectivity. Sociologists Peter Berger, Brigitte Berger, and Hansfried Kellner have examined the ways technology affects how we form beliefs. They call this "the urbanization of consciousness," by which they mean that the modern person living anywhere experiences the same thing that ancient people experienced only in cities—a collision of lifestyles, truth claims, and belief systems. Peter Berger, Brigitte Berger, and Hansfried Kellner, *The Homeless Mind: Modernization and Consciousness* (New York: Vintage, 1973).

2. WRESTLE WITH THE RIGHT ISSUES

Doubt can be disorienting. Disenculturation can't save you from this struggle, but it can focus it in the right places. By differentiating the gospel kernel from the cultural husk, it says, "Wrestle with kernel issues."

When I left my Christian high school, I started struggling with God's judgment. I had been taught the holiness of God and the sinfulness of all people, but befriending thoughtful non-Christians was a surprising experience. They didn't look so bad to me, but the doctrine of judgment suddenly did.

Reflecting on this, I saw that some of what I was wrestling with was biblical and some was merely cultural. Biblically, the New Testament teaches that the Lord will judge the living and the dead by a man whom he has appointed (Acts 17:31; Rom. 2:5–16). Jesus used images like "hell of fire," "weeping and gnashing of teeth," and "outer darkness" to describe being outside his kingdom (Matt. 5:22; 8:12; 22:13). There was no getting around this backdrop to the gospel.

However, some of my revulsion was due to the way judgment had been taught inside evangelical subculture. High-pressure sermons focused more on escaping hell than knowing God. Sin was depicted in grotesque, caricatured forms. The preacher's breath smelled like scorn.

For several years, I tried to relearn what the Bible said (kernel) while tuning out the preachers' voices in my head (husk). I also searched for teachers who explained judgment in a way that didn't dodge the Bible but also didn't sound like these evangelists. Gradually this led to some surprising discoveries. I saw how judgment spoke to my deep longing to live in a world of justice where God makes all things right. I could see this for the first time because I relearned this doctrine *outside* evangelical subculture in a way that addressed my questions and concerns within it.

3. GET INVOLVED IN A CHURCH THAT ENGAGES THE GOSPEL AND CULTURE

Disenculturation shows us it's possible to differentiate the gospel from culture, but it doesn't mean the gospel can be experienced *without any* culture. The whole point of freeing the gospel from one culture is so that it can take root in another. This means that your task is not to find a unicorn culture-free expression of Christianity. Rather, it's to learn and live your faith in your current culture.

Practically, how do you do that? Local churches embody the gospel in a particular culture. Once you've learned to see culture, you can't help but notice that each local church has its own. The best are self-aware. They let the gospel shape the culture *inside* the church. They teach the gospel in a way that connects with the culture *outside* the church. They disciple their members to live *in* that surrounding culture in a distinctly Christlike way.

Look for one of these churches and become involved! A church who loves the gospel *and* the surrounding culture is glad to welcome people who wrestle with hard questions about Christianity. You'll notice it in postures, you'll hear it in sermons, and you'll feel it from leaders.

4. EXPECT TO SEE THE GOSPEL AFRESH

When the gospel is freed from its cultural husk and taken to a new culture, it often shines in fresh and beautiful ways.

One of my favorite examples is a renowned Matt Chandler sermon. Chandler, a pastor in Texas, describes a cringeworthy 1990s youth-ministry event on sexual abstinence. The preacher passes a rose through the audience until it comes back mangled, an analogy for what will happen to those who sleep around. "Now, who would want this rose?" he sneers. Chandler's punchline: "Jesus wants the rose! That's the whole point of the gospel!"

Why is this so powerful to imagine? Because many in Chandler's audience grew up in the evangelical purity movement. They weren't just taught a biblical sex ethic; they were taught it within an environment that relied on fear, pressure, shame, and willpower. Inside this world, the Christian sex ethic sounded like burdensome bad news. Even worse, many who sinned sexually started to feel hopeless, since purity culture tended to obscure God's grace.

How did Chandler know all this? He had stepped outside his subculture. He prefaced the story by telling of a single mom carrying on an extramarital affair. Chandler had befriended her and invited her to the event that night, not knowing it would be a sex sermon. As soon as the preaching started, he knew it would shame his friend and drive her farther from God. Many listening to Chandler's sermon had experienced the same thing. But when Chandler shouts—"Jesus wants the rose!"—he puts purity culture in the "ignore" bucket, and the gospel breaks free to shine in all its beauty.

I know the same benefits of disenculturation are available for you. Don't deconstruct your faith—disenculturate instead.

PART TWO

DECONSTRUCT
THE ISSUES

5

SEX:
TELLING A
BETTER STORY

RACHEL GILSON

On my 18th birthday, I was a committed atheist with a girlfriend, getting ready to head off to Yale College. I was so excited to enter into the real world, away from my small town where I had never felt truly at home. My family had never attended church, even though that was the norm where I grew up. Most of my understanding of Christianity, then, came from the outside. My vision of Christianity—of Jesus— was like an inflated cartoon balloon, stupid bright lines with only air inside. A distraction for children, not to mention dangerous.

That balloon popped during my freshman year. As I felt pain from my failed relationship and insecure because of my brilliant classmates, a certain lecture prompted me to start secretly googling God. After stealing and reading a copy of *Mere Christianity*, I recognized that Jesus was my only hope for life. I repented of my sin, and I believed. I've been following Christ for more than 17 years now, failing and succeeding, learning and unlearning. And as a same-sex-attracted disciple, I've spent a lot of time thinking about the Bible, sexuality, and LGBT+ questions, because that's been my life.

We all come to these conversations with different stories. Maybe like me, you also experience same-sex attraction—but you've grown up in church, and that has strongly influenced your understanding and experience of sexuality. Maybe you still have questions and have heard conflicting answers. Maybe you've felt the need to hide how you feel, or you've experienced mistreatment from others who follow Christ.

Or maybe you only have eyes for the opposite sex, but something hasn't seemed quite right about how Christians have talked about gay and lesbian people. *Is this how Jesus would respond?* Maybe you have friends who identify as gay, or a sibling or cousin who has come out. You've been raised with the idea that gay relationships are wrong, but you've started to wonder if what you've been told stands up to scrutiny. And what does the Bible really say, anyway?

Perhaps you look at how churches have responded to LGBT+ topics and feel disillusioned, wondering if you can trust anything you've heard up to this point. And maybe there are some things you've heard that need to go. Maybe all of us have balloons that need to be popped.

In these few pages, I want to suggest that Jesus has given us in his Word everything we need to discern the fool's gold from the treasure. If we press closer to God and to what he says, we'll be able to break down several false churchy tales about same-sex attraction and sexuality in general that never came from him in the first place. My hope is that on the other side, no matter our attractional patterns, we will be stronger in Jesus Christ. The same humble, truthful love that flows from him in the Gospels flows from him still today.

FALSE TALE 1: IT'S US VS. THEM

Sometimes the way sexuality is discussed makes it seem like same-sex-attracted people are only outside the church. Some of this discussion comes from a good place. There are Christians who long to see the gospel do a good work, and they want to know what it could look like to reach out to LGBT+ people. It can be so easy to discuss a "them" who live outside of the church that some Christians forget, or don't recognize, that part of "us" experiences same-sex attraction, too.

But there is a darker side as well. Some people growing up in churches heard, explicitly and implicitly, a different message: that same-sex attraction is a choice, and people only make that choice if they hate God. Therefore, this experience only exists outside of the church.

Some people do report that they know, at least partially, why they experience same-sex attractions. For many of us, though, our same-sex attractions arose spontaneously, as self-occurring as opposite-sex attraction is for our peers, and just as enduring. In either case, few would describe their same-sex attraction as a choice.

Many children who've gone through Christian education, who've been in our youth groups—or even lived overseas, doing missionary work with their families—have realized that they feel differently than their peers do. But instead of being the safest possible place to understand sexuality, churches have often felt like minefields. One wrong step, one slight giveaway, and it's over.

It doesn't have to be this way. In the Bible, we have God's good news about Jesus Christ, and his good news about our bodies. What if we became churches where youth could grow into understanding why God made us sexual beings, and what it means to say yes to his beauty? What if instead of being paralyzed by the thought that someone could discover our temptations, we could find strength in God's community to build muscles of faith, not fear?

We won't arrive there if we keep up the false story that same-sex attraction is only an experience outside the church. That narrative, along with bullying and worse inside the community of faith, has often made people think that if they continue to feel these desires, they have to leave. We push them into the world, which can only counsel that to be their true selves, they must obey their desires.

But our desires don't own us; Jesus does.

FALSE TALE 2: MARRIAGE IS OUR REWARD

Though it often is pegged to culture alone, the message that we're not full or complete humans unless we're romantically partnered also spreads at church. And at church, that specifically means marriage.

Christians rightly celebrate marriage. God created marriage as a symbol of how he loves the church. Human marriage is supposed to be faithful for life, because God is always faithful to his people, as we should be to him. Human marriage is supposed to be the start of a new household, because God's relationship with his people begins a new family. Human marriage is the only place for sexual intimacy and pleasure, because God's relationship with his people is incredibly intimate and deeply pleasurable. And, if we have ears to hear, human marriage is only to be a male-female union, because the gospel is the picture of two non-interchangeable and different parties, made one by the work of Jesus Christ. Husbands represent Christ, and wives represent his church (Eph. 5:22–33).

Heady stuff, no? Beautiful, too. We're right to celebrate that God has given us this good gift. But we often forget two things.

First, human marriage isn't promised to any of us. It isn't the merit badge you earn for being a good boy or girl, or the capstone of a faithful adolescence. When we've said or implied that it is, we make God look like a liar when he doesn't provide his children with spouses. And we misrepresent the Bible, which especially in the new covenant holds out singleness as a life of dignity, honor, and holiness (1 Cor. 7:6–7, 32–35).

This false promise hurts the whole community and same-sex-attracted believers in particular ways. Some try to force us to become straight and/or married, which has damaged many. Though God does sometimes change people's attractional patterns, even that doesn't mean he promises marriage.

Other people assume that "God wants us to be happy," and because we *don't* usually experience change in our desires, then the Bible must actually teach that God blesses same-sex marriage. After all, if marriage is the prize, and if God isn't mean, then he wouldn't withhold it from us. The very people who should buttress us in costly obedience actually undermine our faithfulness.

Second, marriage is only a signpost gesturing toward reality. When Christ comes, he'll celebrate his wedding with a finally perfect Bride, the church. Whether in life we were married, single, widowed, or abandoned by our spouse—if we're in Christ, we'll all experience that perfect marriage, forever. We're the Bride of Christ, and it *is* a reward: not for our faithfulness, but for his!

The Bible shows that marriages can glorify Christ, and singleness can glorify Christ. Both are challenging and worthy. Both can tell of a coming joy, of which we hear only the outer echoes at an earthly wedding.

FALSE TALE 3: SEXUAL DESIRE IS A PROBLEM

Part of the reason we haven't known how to celebrate singleness is that we haven't known what to do with sexual desire. Marriage has often been the only "solution" churches have to offer, often subtly or directly construing sexuality as a problem.

If sexual desire is a problem, singleness becomes a gauntlet to survive, with threats on every side. In some places where "purity culture" thrives, young women are fed the message that, on the one hand, they constantly tempt their brothers in Christ, so they must police their clothes and motivations strictly. On the other hand, they're catechized to understand that only boys are sexual beings, only boys and bad girls feel desire of any strength. How do you teach a young woman to steward her sexuality if she's not supposed to have one?

Young men aren't given much better. The power of sexual desire isn't denied when it's construed as a problem, but the solutions can seem paltry in comparison. This is where many have done the dance of repression—white knuckles, hoping God will provide a marriage pronto so that they don't have to live long in the misery of waiting.

And what about us same-sex-attracted kids? If the straight kids' desire is coded as hazardous, a ticking time bomb we hope waits to explode until the wedding night, where does that leave us? Is our life supposed to be one long no, without a yes in sight? Is that even possible? Many of us have been taught that waiting isn't supposed to be forever; purity is a possession we protect with our lives, so that we can give that precious gift to our spouse, preferably before the age of 25. But if we suspect we'll never marry, what then?

What if purity isn't something we can lose, because we never had it to begin with? What if sexual desire isn't a mean trick God played on us, but a picture of something holy and righteous?

The reason we have any kind of desire is because we're made in God's image, and he is the ultimate desirer. Existing forever in perfect relationship in the Trinity, he didn't *need* to make humanity. But he wanted to, as a pure overflow of his love and joy. And he continues to desire us, as a good husband desires his bride. Our sexual desire, which we can experience so strongly and so enduringly, is a picture of how much God desires us, and how much we should long for him in return. It is a reminder that all of our lesser desires can point us back to where we will truly be fulfilled.

Now, we shouldn't be naïve. We were born dead in our sins, and our experience and expression of sexuality has been marred by the fall. This is why purity has to be a gift we receive from God daily, not a trophy we preserve from theft. This is also why a chorus of, "No, no, no!" in the face of desire won't be enough to fight sexual sin, nor lead to joy or peace. Like a persistent stream, the waters of our desires will wend and wind until they find an open path.

What if Jesus Christ is that path? What if, as he said, he really is the way (John 14:6)? What if we could learn in a community beloved by God how to see *through* our sexual desires to the God who made them, training ourselves together to say yes to him and no to false lovers? There is room to discipline ourselves for joyful obedience without vilifying the experience of sexual desire, but to instead recognize it as a good gift from God.

CONSTRUCTION ZONE

When I was first feeling drawn to Jesus, I wondered if there'd be a place for someone like me in his church. Initially I was given false hope by friends who told me the Bible doesn't actually say no to same-sex sexuality. But when I read the Bible, I found it does. It took me realizing I wanted Jesus more than any woman to truly come to him, and to find my life in him by losing it (Matt. 10:39).

Some same-sex-attracted youth have made the opposite journey: growing up in the church but feeling like there wasn't room for them. You couldn't play the repression game well enough. You knew your attractions wouldn't change—you'd tried. Constant messaging, maybe even your sins and mistakes, made you feel impure, unworthy, or incapable of marriage. And so you left. Or got pushed out. Many straight kids have had similar experiences.

Other straight kids got out into the wider world and realized the messaging they received at church about "sexual sinners" was off. As you got to know LGBT+ people, you found that some of them, who embraced what the Bible prohibits, actually showed greater kindness, greater empathy, and even greater freedom than you'd been led to think possible. Maybe you decided to "loosen up" too, drawn to the message that expressing your sexuality is the surest way to thrive.

It can be so confusing; what churches have taught can feel backward, hateful, and small. Meanwhile, what the world sells looks full, vibrant, promising. Why not chuck the former and grasp the latter? But it's a false dichotomy; there are many different ways to distort sexuality, and they all lead away from life.

There is a better way, a way of grace *and* truth. Jesus isn't about stereotypes, prejudice, mockery, or hiding. He's about life, forgiveness, strength, and joy. Instead of throwing everything out and walking away, take this as a call to grow in biblical discernment and sift the gold of God's vision for our bodies from the muddy stream of how humanity has soiled sexuality.

With the goodness of God's Word, by the power of God's Spirit, and in the vitality of God's people, we can find this better way together, and share it with others.

6

RACE:
IS CHRISTIANITY A
WHITE MAN'S RELIGION?

CLAUDE ATCHO

The nagging sense that Christianity is the white man's religion is an earnest question—and often an objection—voiced on the block, in the barbershop, and in scholarly debates. With our culture eager to be on the right side of history, this question is no longer exclusive to black folks or other ethnic minorities. White people, especially millennials and Gen Z, are reluctant to embrace a faith that even remotely feels like a tool for past or present oppression.

Whether any of this language describes you—and even if it doesn't—I'm glad you're considering this important question. Done rigorously and honestly, this inquiry can lead you to firm faith.

There are three general reasons that understandably lead people to wonder if Christianity is the white man's religion:

1. History of Oppression. Under the banner of Christianity, African Americans have suffered tremendous pain and evil, from the appalling horrors of chattel slavery to the physical and psychological violence of Jim Crow segregation. How can African Americans embrace the same faith that was complicit with such evil?
2. Whitewashed Jesus. The images of Jesus I saw while growing up—including in my home—was of a European Jesus with blond hair and blue eyes. If the *cornerstone* of Christianity is depicted falsely, is this faith really relevant to the core concerns of black people?
3. Lingering Apathy Toward Racial Justice in the Church. As our broader culture grapples with the deaths of unarmed black people at the hands of police, there is both apathy and hostility toward notions of racial justice throughout the American church. While our world seeks progress on these issues, many churches seem slow to take up the charge.

These reasons tend to overlap and merge. If Christianity has been used to oppress us; if Jesus is essentially European in appearance and concern; if Christians today remain apathetic toward our plight in this life; then isn't Christianity the white man's religion? Can such a faith truly be good for black people?

LEARNING FROM FREDERICK DOUGLASS

While Malcolm X is the black historical figure known for levying the charge that Christianity harms blacks, it's Frederick Douglass roughly a century earlier who best guides us toward an answer.

Douglass was both a Christian and a slave—and later an abolitionist, unparalleled orator, and lay preacher. Douglass had tasted the truth and goodness of Christianity. Yet at the same time, he experienced the physical and psychological trauma of enslavement at the hands of a master who brandished Christianity to legitimize owning him. This dissonance haunted him. We can learn from how Douglass understood both his Christian faith and the abuses inflicted on enslaved people in the name of Christianity.

In the appendix of his first autobiography, filled with unflinching honesty about the suffering he endured at the hands of Christian slave owners, Douglass distinguishes between Christianity in its true essence and Christianity in its abusive distortion. I encourage you to read his words carefully, even if you've heard them before:

> I have, in several instances, spoken in such a tone and manner, respecting religion, as may possibly lead those unacquainted with my religious views to suppose me an opponent of all religion. To remove the liability of such misapprehension, I deem it proper to append the following brief explanation. What I have said respecting and against religion, I mean strictly to apply to the *slaveholding religion* of this land, and with no possible reference to Christianity proper; for, between the Christianity of this land, and the Christianity of Christ, I recognize the widest possible difference—so wide, that to receive the one as good, pure, and holy, is of necessity to reject the other as bad, corrupt, and wicked. To be the friend of the one, is of necessity to be the enemy of the other. I love the pure, peaceable, and impartial Christianity of Christ: I therefore hate the corrupt, slaveholding, women-whipping, cradle-plundering, partial and hypocritical Christianity of this land. Indeed, I can see no reason, but the most deceitful one, for calling the religion of this land Christianity. I look upon it as the climax of all misnomers, the boldest of all frauds, and the grossest of all libels.[1]

Do you hear it? In essence, Douglass provides a 19th-century answer to our question. Christianity isn't the white man's religion, because what his slave owners practiced wasn't biblical Christianity but a distortion condemned by the very Bible they perverted. If you wish to grapple fully with the question of whether Christianity is the white man's religion, then Douglass is a required teacher with a bracing lesson: to answer this question genuinely, you must distinguish between

1.   Frederick Douglass, *Narrative of the Life of Frederick Douglass, An American Slave* (New York: Signet Classics, 1997), 120.

·y of Christ and the Christianity of this land, between
_.⌄uanity proper and its cultural distortions.

Douglass's example and exhortation shows how to *disentangle*
rather than *deconstruct*. Through careful disentangling and patient recovery, we find that Christianity uniquely speaks to the concerns of
black people with experiential and historical foundations that have
empowered our people for centuries.

FAITH THAT CARES FOR BODY AND SOUL

Part of this disentangling and recovering comes from careful attention
to history. Recall that slave owners wouldn't permit major portions
of the Bible to be taught to slaves. Consider that many slave owners
resisted evangelizing slaves and baptizing them in the American colonies, for fear that they would then demand the dignity and equality
befitting all God's image-bearers. Such historical realities highlight
Christianity's innate concern for both soul *and* body, the world to
come *and* the world we inhabit now.

By and large, slave owners knew that enslaved Africans in the colonies would discover, in an uncensored Bible, divine encouragement
and empowerment for their full dignity and liberation. The majority of white Christian denominations understood the stakes: baptism
into full membership in the church would affirm slaves' full humanity
and equality. So slave owners and white churches sought to feed enslaved Africans a distorted faith—a white man's Christianity—since
true Christianity would've disrupted their systems of oppression. Do
you see the horrific irony? They excised large portions of Scripture
and pushed misreadings at the expense of what it actually emphasizes:
God cares for both soul and body and is committed to holiness, righteousness, and justice for all people (Ps. 89:14).

Maybe the Christianity you've experienced is wedded to the functional denial of racism, or the knee-jerk proclamation that all lives
matter, or a general disregard for the plight of black people. Such sen-
timents produce an all-too-real effect: the foreboding sense that when
it comes to the flesh-and-blood concerns of black people, Christianity
has nothing of substantive value to say—it is impotent and silent. The
witness of history is plain: white Christians in America have often

tolerated or participated in slavery, segregation, and racial inequality. While many Christians have fought such evils because of their faith, too many others have twisted their faith into a rationale for maintaining racism's status quo.

This is where Douglass's model of disentangling is vital. The plainest reading of the Scriptures shows us that Christianity is not impotent or silent—it speaks with the God-breathed words that drove our ancestors to seek both spiritual and physical freedom. To a world that often demonizes blackness, assigning an inherent biological or cultural inferiority to those of African descent, Christianity declares all people are made in God's image (Gen. 1:26–28). Those who enslave other people, then, are nothing less than ungodly (1 Tim. 1:10). To those wondering what God desires—and to those who remain apathetic to pressing social issues—the Scriptures call us "to do justice, and to love kindness, and to walk humbly with your God" (Mic. 6:8). To those wondering if God cares for the plight of their people, Christianity gives us Christ himself, who understands suffering, grants salvation, and charges us to love God and to love our neighbor as ourselves. To a world seeking to usher in its sense of perfect justice in the present, Christianity tells us God will do this fully and justly on an appointed day (Acts 17:31). This is good news for all people, and it is a vision of life and faith that speaks to the lingering pain of black experience in America.

You don't have to abandon the faith to critique its abuses of black people—in fact, the greatest critiques against Christianity's distortions is Christianity lived faithfully and Scripture read plainly. Though it has been muzzled and twisted, God's Word continues to speak to our grittiest concerns.

RECOVERING THE TESTIMONY OF OUR ENSLAVED ANCESTORS

The phenomenon of disentangling biblical Christianity from its distortions is the only way to understand one of the most miraculous developments in modern history: enslaved Africans' widespread embrace of the religion of their oppressors. Countless enslaved Africans saw past slave owners' malicious misreadings of Scripture to gaze on—and embrace—the Christian faith. In the very faith misused to dehumanize them, they uncovered God's affirmation of their humanity, his call to seek equality, and his saving revelation in Christ. So they carried their lament, scars, and trauma to heaven's throne. Patiently and prayerfully, they searched the Scriptures and disentangled the true faith from its heinous distortions.

When it comes to the history of Christianity and African Americans, it's understandable to focus on the abuses we've suffered in the name of the faith. There are many. We must reckon with this pain both for our healing and for our learning. But history is emphatic: the story of Christianity and black people is more than a tale of our oppression. It's a story that contains multitudes, a story of suffering and triumph, of unspeakable pain and unshakable faith.

If you're African American or of African descent, you have a great cloud of ethnic witnesses, many of whom tasted suffering but found in the salvation of Jesus and in Scripture transformational hope for this world and the next. Black believers like Martin Luther King Jr., Sojourner Truth, and Fannie Lou Hamer left an indelible mark on history by battling for justice and righteousness because of their faith, not despite it. If you're on the edge of deconstruction—or have already made the leap—recall the cloud of ancestral witnesses who testify of Christ, not because of the coercion of the white man or colonialism, but because Christianity is true and good for all people.

I encourage you to reflect deeply, read prayerfully and widely from voices old and new, and converse communally before writing off the faith that carried our ancestors through harrowing trials with their dignity intact.

AFRICAN ROOTS OF EARLY CHRISTIAN HISTORY

Another concern often arises from African Americans toward this religion of their ancestors. Even if Christianity has helped our people, is it natural to us—or is it just the legacy of colonization?

The massive popularity of Marvel's 2018 *Black Panther* film, and the recent rise of African spiritualities among black millennials, are linked to this question. Both reflect, in different ways, a growing desire among younger African Americans to recover their ethnic heritage—to "decolonize" from beliefs that prize Eurocentric cultural norms and return to one's African or ancestral roots. Religious groups like the Black Hebrew Israelites capitalize on this impulse by claiming to offer a religious identity natural to African Americans, unstained by white people and the abuses of Christianity.

Of course, God loves ethnic diversity, designing and prizing it to the point of including it in the renewal of heaven and earth (Rev. 7:9). But this is not merely a matter of future hope—just look at Christianity's origins, specifically in Africa. You don't need to abandon Christianity to discover your African heritage; you need to discover Christianity's African roots.

Consider that one of the three epicenters of early Christianity was Alexandria, located in Egypt. Many of the most formative Christian figures were African, from seminal theologians like Tertullian to Augustine to the faithful female martyr Perpetua. Christianity in Africa long predates chattel slavery and European colonialism. Places like Ethiopia and Sudan were home to thriving Christianity as early as the fourth century. The late scholar Thomas Oden put it powerfully: "Cut Africa out of the Bible and Christian memory, and you have misplaced many pivotal scenes of salvation history. It is the story of the children of Abraham in Africa; Joseph in Africa; Moses in Africa; Mary, Joseph and Jesus in Africa; and shortly thereafter Mark, and Perpetua and Athanasius, and Augustine in Africa."[2]

SAVIOR WHO CARES AND KNOWS

Historical and biblical answers to the haunting question of whether Christianity is a white man's religion are important. But this question isn't resolved through information alone. We're not brains on a stick, after all; we're creatures of desire, led by our hearts, which means our motives and impulses are knots of complexity and brokenness that require careful reflection. So as you wrestle with the question behind this chapter, will you interrogate the cultural narrative and heart impulses that make you think Christianity belongs to whiteness?

2. Thomas C. Oden, *How African Shaped the Christian Mind: Rediscovering the African Seedbed in Western Christianity* (Downers Grove, IL: InterVarsity Press, 2007), 14.

The image of white Jesus is so off-putting because it suggests that Jesus doesn't understand or identify with any of us of non-Anglo descent. Yet Jesus himself drew near to those whom the world forgot and despised. Jesus himself felt the horrifying sting of injustice and suffering. Jesus himself suffered for our sake. There is no other religious figure who can so empathize with the pain and grit of human experience, including the story of African Americans over the centuries.

I urge you to freshly examine Jesus of Nazareth, as revealed in the Gospels, the singular figure who by his unjust suffering, his solidarity with the lowly, and his sacrificial love has been the living proof to our people that Christianity doesn't belong to the white man, but to the risen God-man. He is the ultimate proof that God knows us, sees us, and loves us.

7

POLITICS: JUST SERVANT, TYRANNICAL MASTER

SAMUEL JAMES

In the unfinished basement of our church on a Wednesday night, my friend Robby turned to me and asked, "Do you think it's sinful to not vote for George W. Bush?" It was 2004, and Robbie and I were as conscious as everyone else of the U.S. election. To someone else it may have seemed a strange question, but not to me, and not to anyone else present that evening. The idea that one candidate could represent *the* Christian option was, if not something Robby and I had fully contemplated, certainly something we assumed—probably because it was something our parents and church teachers assumed before us.

Not every Christian is distressed by being raised to hold certain beliefs about faith and politics, then rethinking those beliefs later. But some experience this tension as if they need to deconstruct everything they've known. Sometimes politics devours the theological, leaving a particularly thick wreckage behind.

JUST SERVANT, TYRANNICAL MASTER

Politics is a just servant but a tyrannical master.

Biblically speaking, politics is necessary ultimately because human beings are created in God's image. Human flourishing requires the ability and willingness of God's image-bearers to live in joyful, loving harmony with him and with the created order. Being created in God's image means being created under a divine mandate to take holy dominion over the universe.

Politics is the *how* of holy dominion.

But we need to understand something important. Politics—the just and righteous exercising of power over human institutions—is only a how. It's not a *why*. According to biblical Christianity, politics can only ever be a means to an end, not an end in itself. Before anything political was, God is.

American Christians especially need to be reminded that politics can be a righteous servant, but a tyrannical and blasphemous master. Many churches in the United States maintain a more sustainable sense of unity over their favorite political parties and candidates than the basic doctrines of their Christian faith. In too many churches, members can't articulate even simple points of the gospel, but a Facebook post about an election can draw lines and tear people apart.

Inside many of these churches, the how of politics has dethroned the why of Christianity. I've seen white Christians accuse a black Christian, who shares fundamental doctrinal commitments of Christianity, of being a "liberal" simply because he speaks of experiencing police injustice. He didn't say anything unbiblical—on the contrary, the Bible assumes that fallen humans will wield power unjustly. He simply failed to toe an earthly partisan line.

This is what it looks like when God's people allow politics to master them spiritually, emotionally, and theologically. But politics is just like any other idol: it doesn't deliver what it promises. That's why many of the most politically conscious people you know are also the most anxious, the most fearful, the most volatile. The idol of politics promises a feeling of control over this intimidating world. In reality, though, it amplifies fear by keeping our eyes off the Sovereign ruler of history.

IDOLATRY ON BOTH SIDES

It's not hard for me to see how politics can become idolatry when I'm looking at *other*s. I can spot a speck of tribalism in the eyes of Those Kinds of Christians from a mile away. But the same idolatry can and does take root in the hearts of those who think they are rejecting it.

Deconstructing your Christian faith out of frustration with your church or your parents' political commitments is itself a form of this idolatry. Just as holding up the Republican Party platform as a test of Christian fellowship is wrong, using politics as a reason to abandon biblical commitments is likewise wrong. It's the same error, just in a different direction.

My friend Jesse (not his real name) was, like me, raised in a very conservative homeschooling environment that taught evangelical theology alongside strongly right-wing politics. In time, Jesse realized that much of what he was taught about America's two political parties wasn't always true. Because of this, he started questioning not only his parents' politics but also their belief in things like the inerrancy of Scripture, substitutionary atonement, and the exclusivity of Christ.

Over the last few years, I've watched with fascination as Jesse has become confident in his new progressive theology and politics. A while back his Facebook posts were more questioning, simply trying to "start a conversation" and defuse the swaggering confidence of his fundamentalist family members. Today his posts about both politics and theology are much bolder. He believes substitutionary atonement is a morally outrageous doctrine. He has no interest in hearing from people who oppress women by holding to male-only eldership. With a sharp wit, he puts down anybody who could be so morally corrupt as to support certain candidates.

Jesse may have thrown off the conservative politics he was raised to believe his faith demanded. But from where I'm sitting, Jesse is still ensnared in political idolatry. His politics still dictate his faith—just in the opposite direction from his parents.

For younger Christians in particular, it's easy to *say* the Bible transcends our politics when what we really mean is the Bible transcends *your* politics. It's easy to feel like we're better off simply because we swing, like a pendulum, in the opposite direction from the mistakes of those who formed us. That's human nature. The trouble with pendulums is that all they do is move back and forth.

Wisdom looks different.

WINNING VS. WISDOM

Wisdom isn't merely running in the opposite direction of those we dislike. In a polarized society that's allergic to quiet, careful thinking, it's easy to think that wisdom needs to feel like winning. This is the air Westerners breathe. Politicians, activists, and even many pastors carefully shape their rhetoric to make everything their opponents do look as bad as possible.

When we imbibe this kind of thinking day after day—as we'll inevitably do if we spend hours every week consuming news and social media—we're being formed into the kind of people C. S. Lewis warned about in his essay "The Inner Ring."

In this essay, Lewis observes that one of the most intense temptations is to believe and behave merely for the sake of being approved in our various groups and cliques. Addressing a group of young university students, Lewis warns that the willingness to sacrifice principles and morality for membership isn't something that will stop if they can only once find the right inner ring to join. If they give in to it, they will make continual, increasingly unthinkable compromises, because there will always be one more inner circle to desire. "Of all the passions," Lewis says, "the passion for the Inner Ring is most skillful in making a man who is not yet a very bad man do very bad things."[1]

---

1.   C. S. Lewis, "The Inner Ring," in *The Weight of Glory and Other Addresses* (New York: Harper-Collins, 2001), 153–54.

When it comes to Christians and politics, far too often the question that rules the day is not, "Is this, according to what God has said in Scripture, true, good, and beautiful?" Instead, it is, "What are My Kind of People saying about this?" or even worse, "What are the Wrong Kind of People saying about this (because the opposite must be true)?"

This is what happens when right-wing Christians make peace with cruelty toward immigrant children because it "owns the libs." This is what happens when left-wing Christians fail to speak up for the unborn because doing so would put them alongside people they dislike. When it's winning that matters and not wisdom, people outsource their convictions to keep their tribe.

On the other hand, if you let the Bible shape your conscience, you don't have to keep track of where your views will sort you. The Bible that insists on the personhood of the unborn and the immorality of murder is the same Bible that says God looks carefully at how a society treats its orphans, widows, and poor. The Bible that commands the people of God to show compassion to the vulnerable and kindness to the stranger is the same Bible that promises divine wrath for those who reject our Creator's design for sexuality and gender. The Bible that teaches salvation is only in Jesus Christ also teaches that all of us, saved or lost, are made in his image.

This is the wisdom that the gospel offers. If you embrace this wisdom, you probably won't "win" much, because you won't easily map onto our polarized public square. Biblical wisdom will at times get you called a liberal by those on the right or a fundamentalist by those on the left: somewhat like how Jesus was savagely rejected and maligned by stiff, moralistic religious leaders, but also rejected by common folk who didn't like what he said about their need for him (John 8:31–59).

While throwing off what you were told in church youth group may feel like achieving a kind of independence, in reality you're probably just swinging like a pendulum toward another authority source: new friends, new professors, new social-media accounts, or new books or articles. The question is not, "Will you shape yourself or will you allow someone to shape you?" The question is, "Will you be shaped by an all-powerful, all-merciful Creator who loves justice and righteousness and mercy? Or will you be shaped by the endless parade of fads and tribes?"

To truly have a faith that transcends (not ignores) politics means embracing an authentically Christ-shaped approach.

NEW IDENTITY

Humility is so rare in political discourse because, for many people, political belief and belonging constitute the core of their identity. Disagreement becomes equivalent to attack, and exposure to beliefs that challenge us is no longer appreciated as something that can strengthen us.

In their book *The Coddling of the American Mind*, Greg Lukianoff and Jonathan Haidt present compelling data that show younger Americans in particular are allergic to contrary ideas and people. The deep problems of polarization and demonization in contemporary culture owe first and foremost to how today's emerging adults were taught, as children, to think of themselves. If children are taught to think of themselves as "fragile," if they're taught to always trust what their feelings tell them, and if they're taught that the world is a simple battle between good and bad people, then they will grow up unable to see those who disagree with them as anything but dangers.[2]

The decrepit state of much of our public square owes, Haidt and Lukianoff conclude, to how we think of ourselves.

They're right. Yet their analysis doesn't go far enough. The truth is that without the transcendent truth claims of the Bible, we're all left to ourselves in forming our identities, and these identities *are* extremely fragile—since we can't control the world. The only way out of the fragility that gives rise to hatred and avoidance of others is to believe that we (and the universe) don't finally belong to us, but to God.

When you're confident in the deepest parts of your soul that the sovereign Jesus Christ is reigning over the world, and that he has died and risen to keep you safe in his presence forever, fear and loathing toward those who disagree with you loses its power. You can try to

2.   Greg Lukianoff and Jonathan Haidt, *The Coddling of the American Mind: How Good Intentions and Bad Ideas Are Setting Up a Generation for Failure* (New York: Penguin, 2018), 177.

persuade others with gentleness instead of seeing them as cosmic bad guys who are going to wreck everything unless they're stopped.

Before you deconstruct your Christian faith, consider whether any identity you can craft for yourself out of political beliefs can actually make you both courageous and compassionate. Jesus can make you like that, because he is like that.

RIGHT WORSHIP

A faith that goes beyond politics is centered on worship. You may ask, "What does worship have to do with politics?" The answer is: everything.

An evangelical church in the Bible Belt, compromising what the Bible says about justice in order to keep in step with its preferred political tribe? That's a worship issue. A 20-something college student who rejects Jesus's claims because she can't imagine condemning people who want to live out their free sexual preferences and identities? That's a worship issue. What happens when politics and faith collide reveals something fundamental about our worship.

In the absence of worshiping God as he's revealed himself in Jesus Christ, the human heart reaches for idols. Again, it's almost impossible to overstate how common the worship of politics has become for Americans, including many Christians. One jarring example of how politics has become a god in our culture is a survey from 2019 indicating "both Republicans and Democrats would be more upset if their child married a person of the opposing political party than if they married a person of a different religious faith."[3]

When you forget that God controls the universe, and that he orchestrates all of it toward final justice and goodness, you will see those who disagree with your politics as not just wrong, but *evil*. And your hostile reaction probably reveals that your deepest trust isn't in the power of Christ but in the power of the ballot.

From this angle, you can see how walking away from the person, work, and promises of Jesus Christ—because he doesn't fit your po-

---

3.   David French, "Politics Is a Jealous God," The French Press, December 29, 2019, https://frenchpress.thedispatch.com/p/politics-is-a-jealous-god

litical preferences—is utter madness. Abandoning Christ won't make your politics more tolerant and sophisticated. What it will do, in all likelihood, is surrender you to the whims of a secular outrage and cancel culture that is ruthless and unforgiving. It'll leave you without a moral foundation. Worst of all, it'll rob you of the only hope steady enough to survive deep suffering, unmet expectations, shattered dreams, powerful enemies, and broken trust. Only Christ is big enough to assure you of ultimate hope, because only Christ is big enough to one day undo everything broken about this world.

DUSTBIN OF HISTORY

No political party has a trademark on the truth claims of Jesus Christ. If being a Christian means anything at all, it means believing that Jesus is truly, unchangeably in authority over all human activities and institutions. His death and resurrection demanded responses long before the United States of America existed. And his death and resurrection will demand a response long after you, I, and what we know as the world today has been forgotten and swept into the dustbin of history.

Instead of looking at other Christians and deciding how to respond to Jesus, look at Jesus. Look at his wisdom, his compassion, his excellence. Look at his patience and righteousness and kingship. Look at his extravagant promises of grace and his mighty guarantee of a final justice. Then after you look at him, look at the world around you: left, right, and center. Look at the brokenness, the hypocrisy, the inconsistency of the City of Man. Look at what life is like when sinful people try to rule the world apart from their Creator.

If you look at Jesus and then the world, sincerely *wanting* to see, then you *will* see. And you won't be the same.

8

INTERNET: DECONSTRUCTING FAITH ONLINE

JAY Y. KIM

A few years ago we were preparing for the arrival of our second child. On my to-do list was to move a crib from our firstborn's room into what would become our newborn's room. The crib was too large to fit through the doorway, so disassembly was required. There was one problem. This particular crib required specific tools, which I'd neglected to keep. After an hour of delicately twisting screws with ill-fitted instruments, frustration got the best of me. In a momentary lapse of judgment, I lifted a hammer high above like Thor ready to rain thunder, before I caught myself.

Whether a crib or the Christian faith, there are always two ways to deconstruct—with hammers or with precise tools.

Deconstructing with hammers is quick and easy. But it's also reckless. The resulting mess leaves us with little from which to reconstruct anything of substance. Deconstructing with precise tools, meanwhile, is much more methodical. It's rarely as quick and easy as the hammer. But we retain the materials needed to reconstruct something of substance in the end.

Many deconstruction stories in recent years share an alarming trend: the strong influence of online caricatures of Christianity. Maybe this is your story. If it is, I understand. A quick scroll through the social-media landscape exposes us to plenty of troubling renderings of Christianity. Social media are adept at plunging us into echo chambers designed to infuriate us, for this is how they keep us clicking and swiping. As Arthur Brooks notes, "On any contentious subject, [social-media] platforms are contempt machines."[1]

I, too, am often exasperated by the online content of many who claim to follow Christ. But when caricatures of Christianity become the primary motivation for deconstruction, we can unwittingly disassemble faith with hammers. The caricatures fuel our contempt. Outrage overwhelms, and we swing away. When we're done, only fragments of our former faith remain. This is tragic.

But there is another way, a path paved by wisdom, Scripture, and the church. This path requires us to come out from hiding behind digital walls, to engage real people in the real world. It's a journey of tools handled with precision, not hammers wielded in rage.

WIT OR WISDOM?

The internet overflows with wit, a never-ending stream of clever, attention-grabbing morsels of amusement and (mis)information. Its public expression always appears sudden and spontaneous, even if it was crafted laboriously over time. This is wit's nature. If it isn't jarringly abrupt, then it isn't witty. It makes logical sense, then, that on-

---

1.   Arthur C. Brooks, *Love Your Enemies: How Decent People Can Save America from the Culture of Contempt* (New York: HarperCollins, 2019), 24.

line spaces are dominated by wit. As our digital experiences grow in speed, making us less and less patient, our appetites change. What we crave are the jarringly abrupt morsels. Slow and steady give way to quick and easy.

But while wit rules the day in the digital age, Christian faith points us to a distinctly different virtue: wisdom (Prov. 3:13; 4:5; 8:11). Wisdom, though, isn't quick and easy. It's not a swipe or push of a button away, but "far off . . . and very deep" (Eccles. 7:23–25). Wisdom is difficult to find. There are no shortcuts, no abbreviated versions. Nothing could be more diametrically opposed to the way we most often spend our time online. Daniel Grothe astutely points out one of our greatest challenges to seeking and finding wisdom today: "We are a society being buzzed, zapped, and alerted to death. Words litter the landscape of our lives like chaff on a threshing floor."[2]

Wisdom is difficult at best (and impossible at worst) to find in a grabby headline or pristinely filtered photo. Again, that's the territory of wit. And in the digital age, so much deconstruction is spurred on by wit rather than wisdom. Assorted voices pop up on our feeds. They grab our attention with pithy statements dissecting faith. Then the algorithms do their magic and send us spiraling into a cacophony of like-minded voices. Before we know it, our faith is coming undone.

But truncated, oversimplified renderings leave little room for the complexity, depth, and nuance required to arrive at a substantive understanding of genuine Christian faith. So rather than allowing wit to win the day, pursue biblical wisdom. And what does biblical wisdom look like, exactly? "Wisdom from above is first pure, then peaceable, gentle, open to reason, full of mercy and good fruits, impartial and sincere" (James 3:17).

This sort of wisdom is strikingly different from many online versions of "Christianity." I've found it tremendously beneficial to focus on the influence of wise mentors in my life, above and before Christian influencers online. Wise mentors are almost always found in em-

---

2.   Daniel Grothe, *Chasing Wisdom: The Lifelong Pursuit of Living Well* (Nashville: Thomas Nelson, 2020), 98. For another insightful treatment on wisdom, see Brett McCracken, *The Wisdom Pyramid: Feeding Your Soul in a Post-Truth World* (Wheaton, IL: Crossway, 2021).

bodied communities rather than social media. And often, they look nothing like what you'd expect.

Look for those who've eschewed spectacle for steadiness; who've been faithful—to God, family, church, friends—over a long period of time; who've learned a lot but still hunger to learn; who find joy in simplicity; who remain composed in the face of obstacles; who are more generous than most people know; who delight in Scripture; who love and follow Jesus in all of the big, little, and in-between stuff of life.

TRANSCENDING THE EXTREMES

As you seek wise mentors, you'll notice some things. Those who've sought and found wisdom are quick to listen, slow to speak, and rarely are caught in the fickleness of cultural tides. They're tempered, thoughtful, and almost always at peace, even when slighted or wronged. Our online experiences are anything but. Online, I'm often quick to speak, slow to listen, and drowning in culture's fickle waters. Maybe you can relate. This is the currency of the digital age—extremes equal clicks. Too many of us embark on deconstruction from online extremes. But this is unwise: we need distance to achieve clarity. We need to transcend the extremes.

What does it mean to transcend the extremes, practically speaking? There are several ways, but one of the most important, especially in our over-informed and so-often-misinformed age, is to immerse ourselves in Scripture. This is of course easier said than done. Ironically, one of the reasons diving deeply into Scripture is so difficult is that our online tendencies deteriorate our aptitude. As we scroll, swipe, and click away, neurological pathways are rewired. We're losing the ability to engage long-format texts. Instead, we long to consume information the way the internet delivers it: in truncated bursts. As the writer Nicholas Carr puts it, "Once I was a scuba diver in the sea of words. Now I zip along the surface like a guy on a Jet Ski."[3]

It's no wonder online extremes are fueling so much deconstruction. When reading the Bible in truncated bursts, we'll inevitably ex-

3.   Nicholas Carr, *The Shallows: What the Internet Is Doing to Our Brains* (New York: W. W. Norton & Company, 2011), 7.

perience a shallow substitute of genuine faith. Some of Christianity's most ardent modern critics read the Bible this way. Take, for example, atheist Richard Dawkins: "The God of the Old Testament is arguably the most unpleasant character in all fiction: jealous and proud of it; a petty, unjust, unforgiving control-freak; a vindictive, bloodthirsty ethnic cleanser; a misogynistic, homophobic, racist . . . bully."[4]

The only way to arrive at this conclusion is to read the Bible as disconnected, bite-sized bits of data. But when we read and study more deeply, this depiction of God becomes a shallow and misinformed caricature built from taking select verses out of context. So before you deconstruct, I invite you to transcend the extremes by reading Scripture—slowly, deeply, immersively. Before turning to social media to form an opinion, turn to the primary source, the Bible, and journey there long enough for God to form you. Study it in community—find others who regularly plumb its depths and join them. This is when the wise mentor can be a tremendous resource.

FOLLOWERS, FRIENDS, FAMILY

I'm an only child, and my mother worked multiple jobs when I was a boy. Essentially, I grew up alone, which meant everything was about me. Sometimes the internet reminds me of my childhood. While MySpace is no longer the cultural phenomenon it was in the early 2000s, our digital experiences continue to be about *my space*. We customize to our preferences. Blocking, unfriending, and canceling anything or anyone that doesn't suit us just right is as easy as a click or a swipe. On the internet we're often only children.

I'm now the parent of two young children. Watching them navigate life together is fascinating. Sibling relationships are volatile and unpredictable. But kinship isn't. Kinship is undeniable, unceasing, and unchanging. My children are forever brother and sister. They're inextricably connected. They didn't choose each other. The only choice they have is how they will cultivate their kinship.

There's no denying that Christian community is difficult. Because the church is made up of sinful people like you and me, she is flawed.

---

4.   Richard Dawkins, *The God Delusion* (Boston: Houghton Mifflin Harcourt, 2006), 51.

Maybe you've been hurt by the church. If so, you're not alone. I'm right there with you. And when I've been hurt, I've so often been tempted to block, unfriend, cancel, and begin to deconstruct. But this familiar reaction is born out of a grave misunderstanding about what the church actually is.

On social media, we're primarily followers and friends. We follow personalities, and we connect with friends. But these online relationships are established on our terms. We choose people to follow and to befriend, based mostly on personal interest and self-gain. We have the power to sever these relationships and dictate their terms. But Christians are called to a much deeper sort of relationship; not to follow personalities or make some friends, but to be family. Remember, there is no choice in the matter of family. We're inextricably connected. We didn't choose each other. The only choice we have is how we'll cultivate our kinship.

When we see the church simply as a place to find a personality to follow or some people to befriend, severing ties becomes a readily available and tempting option. But the church is family—by faith in Jesus, we become children of God and part of his family (see John 1:12–13; 1 John 3:1a). What binds us is much stronger and more significant than the nonchalance of our digital associations.

Family is messy, to be sure. The call to live as brothers and sisters isn't an invitation into some enchanted utopia, where everyone smiles and gets along merrily. Church is messy. There is no perfect church for any of us. That idea is a unicorn, a wishful thought. As Dietrich Bonhoeffer writes, "Those who love their dream of a Christian community more than the Christian community itself become destroyers of that Christian community even though their personal intentions may be ever so honest, earnest, and sacrificial."[5]

5.   Dietrich Bonhoeffer, *Life Together and Prayerbook of the Bible* (Minneapolis: Fortress Press, 2008), 36. As Sam Allberry puts it, "The only perfect church is the heavenly assembly, and this does not meet at 10:30 a.m. each Sunday a short drive from your house. So until you're called to join the throng around God's throne, you're called to belong to a church in which others will get things wrong—and so will you." Sam Allberry, *Why Bother with Church?: And Other Questions About Why You Need It and Why It Needs You* (Purcellville, VA: The Good Book Company, 2016), 73.

When we're unwilling to walk patiently alongside the family God has called us to, we destroy that family, to borrow Bonhoeffer's words. In the end, all is in shambles. So what might be a more effective approach, when patience wears thin and we're tempted to throw faith out along with the family? Rather than fleeing at the first sign of agitation or annoyance, stay. Be kind, tenderhearted, and forgiving (Eph. 4:32). Pursue unity, sympathize, and be humble (1 Pet. 3:8). Rejoice and weep with those who rejoice and weep (Rom. 12:15). Suffer alongside others (1 Cor. 12:26) and bear their burdens (Gal. 6:2). Do this steadily enough, and the agitation and annoyance will eventually ease. As we learn the stories behind the stories of our brothers and sisters, even those who once seemed a nuisance, empathy will gradually grow. We'll begin to see that for all her flaws, the church is our family, kinfolk to whom we eternally belong.

DECONSTRUCTING CARICATURES

During my early college years, I went through a deconstruction of my faith. This was in part because no one seemed to have adequate answers for my questions, and in part because the church had unknowingly inflicted some emotional wounds. So I walked away, from the church and from faith.

Then, in my early 20s, a group of guys, faithful followers of Jesus, invited me to a weekly Monday night hangout. We ate pizza, played video games, and talked honestly. They welcomed my questions. They offered wisdom in the big and little things of life. They invited me to study Scripture with them, opening my eyes to see and experience the text in new ways. They bore my burdens. They rejoiced with me and wept with me. Soon enough, they'd taken the hammer I was using to deconstruct faith, and we were now using far more helpful precision tools together to deconstruct the caricatures.

This is my hope and prayer for you, that the blinding lights of online caricatures would succumb to the light of Christ; that God would guide you toward others who've traversed the dark valleys of doubt you now face, with his Word as a lamp to your feet and light to your path (Ps. 119:105). And that through their stories and their lives, you might see and experience genuine faith anew.

9

SOCIAL JUSTICE: BREAKUP OR BREAKTHROUGH?

THADDEUS WILLIAMS

Have you ever felt like many Christian churches today don't care about justice the way they should, like they're on the "wrong side of history"? Maybe you've even felt like that has become a deal-breaker for you, that your passion for a more just world could be more deeply gratified if you simply cut ties with the church, with all of its baggage and blind spots. If you've been burned by hypocrisy in the church or love someone who has, then perhaps that impulse to bail has grown irresistible.

The conclusion that Christianity is hardly the beacon of social justice it should be is a common theme in many deconstruction stories.

If this thought applies to you or someone you know, let me offer five questions for self-reflection. But first a brief disclaimer. Combining the word "social" with the word "justice" is a bit like mixing Mentos with soda. It is highly explosive, especially when we don't bother to define our terms. Movements as diverse as labor unions, gay-rights groups, and the American Nazi Party all claim the banner of social justice. While I unpack the different definitions in detail in my recent book,[1] for our purposes let's keep a simple distinction in mind. Social Justice A is the kind of justice that is deeply compatible with a biblical worldview and Social Justice B is not. With that distinction in place, let's ask our five questions.

QUESTION 1: AS I SEEK SOCIAL JUSTICE, HAVE I DISTINGUISHED A BREAKUP FROM A BREAKTHROUGH?

Others in this book have pointed out that many people deconstruct not from actual Christianity but from some short-sighted counterfeit. This certainly rings true of the friends I've known who've claimed to "break up" with God and the Christian faith over questions of social justice. If you're considering breaking up with a version of Christianity that turns a blind eye to injustices here on earth, then you're not breaking up with Christianity but with neo-Gnosticism—what Francis Schaeffer called "super-spirituality"[2] disguised as Christianity. We should all be dismayed by a head-in-the-clouds Christianity in which the work of Christ has no implications for injustice in the here and now. The lordship of Christ, as Abraham Kuyper preached, stretches over "every square inch in the whole terrain of human existence."[3] As one of my favorite poets, Evangeline Paterson, writes, "I was brought up in a Christian environment where, because God had to be given preeminence, nothing else was allowed to be important. I have

---

1. *Confronting Injustice without Compromising Truth: 12 Questions Christians Should Ask About Social Justice* (Grand Rapids, MI: Zondervan, 2020).

2. See Francis Schaeffer, *The New Super-Spirituality* (Downers Grove, IL: InterVarsity, 1973).

3. *Abraham Kuyper: A Centennial Reader*, ed. James D. Bratt (Grand Rapids, MI: Eerdmans, 1998), 488.

broken through to the position that because God exists, everything has significance."[4]

Consider one possibility for reframing your experience. What if what feels like a *breaking up* is, in reality, a *breaking through*? What if your concerns for justice are precisely the kind of breakthrough Paterson describes? What if they are a sign that you are outgrowing a neo-Gnostic "Christianity," that you are growing more deeply in sync with the God of the Bible who stands in deep solidarity with the oppressed (Prov. 17:5) and commands us to seek justice (Mic. 6:8; Isa. 58:6–10; Isa. 1:15–17)?

QUESTION 2: AS I SEEK SOCIAL JUSTICE, AM I BREAKING FROM A ONE-SIDED STEREOTYPE OF CHRISTIANITY?

If I were raised deep in the Amazonian jungles, and then suddenly dropped in the middle of Los Angeles and handed a smartphone and a Twitter account, I'd draw some clear conclusions about Christianity—namely, Christians are bigots, phobics, and haters. Christians have declared war on women, they're fond of white supremacy, they don't care for the poor, they hate Muslims and gay people, are the greatest oppressors on earth, and have been for centuries. This is a common caricature of Christianity in many Social Justice B circles.

We need to set some facts straight to see through social-media stereotypes and partisan propaganda. Here is a mere snippet of relevant facts:

- Christians rescued the unwanted babies who had been tossed away like garbage at the human dumps of the Roman Empire, usually simply for being female, and adopted them as cherished children.[5]
- Christians built more hospitals and orphanages to serve the suffering than any other movement in history, while offering a ro-

4. Joy Alexander, "In Conversation with Evangeline Paterson," *Journal of the Irish Christian Study Centre,* vol. 4 (1989): 42.
5. See Thaddeus Williams, *Reflect: Becoming Yourself by Mirroring the Greatest Person in History* (Bellingham, WA: Lexham, 2018), 123–25.

bust framework for human rights and human sexuality that has brought freedom and dignity to millions.[6]

- Christians inspired skyrocketing literacy rates around the world, even introducing written languages into cultures that had none and spearheading linguistic breakthroughs in modern English, French, and German.[7]
- Christians directly inspired universities into existence, including St. Andrews, Oxford, Cambridge, Harvard, Princeton, and many more, along with sparking the Scientific Revolution under the conviction that science exists "to the glory of God and the benefit of the human race."[8]
- Christians organized resistance movements against the Nazis. The Christian village of Le Chambon in Southern France hid and saved thousands of Jews fleeing from Hitler's SS.[9]
- Christians led the movement to abolish slavery not only in America and the United Kingdom but also in India, Africa, the Middle East, and South America.[10]

Believers practicing Social Justice A and serving their communities aren't mere relics of the past. A 2018 study in the United States found that practicing Christians outpace all other groups in providing food to the poor, donating clothing and furniture to the poor, praying for the poor, giving personal time to serve the poor in their communities, and serving those beyond American borders.[11] A recent study

6.   See Francis Schaeffer, *A Christian Manifesto* (Wheaton, IL: Crossway, 2005), Kyle Harper, *From Shame to Sin: The Christian Transformation of Sexual Morality in Late Antiquity* (Cambridge, MA: Harvard University Press, 2016), and Brian Tierney, *The Idea of Natural Rights* (Grand Rapids: Eerdmans, 1997).

7.   See Rodney Stark, *The Victory of Reason: How Christianity Led to Freedom, Capitalism, and Western Success* (New York: Random House, 2005).

8.   See Ian Barbour, *Religion and Science: Historical and Contemporary Issues* (San Francisco: HarperCollins, 1997), 3–32.

9.   See Thaddeus Williams, *Love, Freedom, and Evil: Does Authentic Love Require Free Will?* (New York: Brill, 2011), 43–55.

10. See Tom Holland, *Dominion: How the Christian Revolution Remade the World* (New York: Basic Books, 2019), and Thomas Sowell, *Black Rednecks and White Liberals* (New York: Encounter, 2006), 112–23.

11. "Three Reasons to Have Hope about Global Poverty," Barna Research Group, April 26, 2018, https://www.barna.com/research/3-reasons-hope-global-poverty.

by a nonreligious research group looked at a dozen faith communities around Philadelphia. With a 54-point metric to determine the economic effect of these congregations on their surrounding communities, researchers found that a dozen congregations generated $50,577,098 in economic benefit to their neighborhoods in a single year.[12] Further, Christian communities today excel in adoption, foster parenting, fighting human trafficking, and community development.[13]

"Sure," comes the welcome skeptic's reply, "but didn't Christians also instigate crusades, inquisitions, witch burnings, and other atrocities?" Sadly, yes. But which self-proclaimed believers do you think merit the name "Christian"—the ones dignifying or the ones dehumanizing their neighbors? Don't buy into the false either-or. It isn't a matter of *either* remaining a Christian *or* leaving the historic faith to pursue justice. Instead, carry the torch of a long history of Christian Social Justice A and participate in vibrant contemporary churches that love the oppressed precisely because they love Jesus. That isn't a break*up* with Christianity but a break*through* into a rich Christian tradition in which God's command (not suggestion) to "seek justice" (Isa. 1:17) is taken seriously.

QUESTION 3: AS I SEEK SOCIAL JUSTICE, AM I TAKING THE DECONVERSION STORIES OF OTHER CHRISTIANS SERIOUSLY?

It's common to hear stories of people who walk away from the faith because they find biblical Christianity too stifling and judgmental, lacking in true justice. But there are beautiful stories that move the opposite direction. Some find deep liberation when they deconstruct today's trending Social Justice B ideologies and discover the justice-in-

12. David O'Reilly, "A Study Asks: What's the Churches Economic Worth?," *Philadelphia Inquirer*, February 1, 2011, https://www.inquirer.com/philly/news/religion/20110201_A_study_asks__What_s_a_church_s_economic_worth_.html.

13. Also contradicting the narrative that Christians are typically on the wrong side of today's trendy oppressor-oppressed narrative, we find that "Christian persecution and genocide is worse now than 'any time in history.'" This includes being targeted, imprisoned, beaten, raped, hanged, crucified, and bombed for claiming Jesus as Lord. Every month an average of 345 Christians are killed for their faith, 105 churches or Christian buildings are burned or attacked, and 219 Christians are detained without trial. "Persecution According to the Bible," Open Doors USA, https://www.opendoorsusa.org/what-is-persecution.

spiring truths of the historic Christian faith. In the words of Monique Duson, founder and director of the Center for Biblical Unity, "With [my] constant focus on evil systems, I had become oblivious to the evil in my own heart. . . . According to historic Christianity, salvation is the good news of Jesus's life, death, and resurrection so sinners of all colors can be saved by a free act of divine grace. [My ideology] had pulled me away from that good news into a social justice gospel in which the finished work of Jesus wasn't enough."[14] In the words of Edwin Ramirez,

> I did not realize how much resentment I harbored. . . . Then the Lord opened my eyes and set me free in an unexpected place, a rural, predominantly white church. . . . Scanning the room, my eyes fell on an older lady whose face was filled with joy as she worshiped our God. Then it hit me: "That older white lady is my sister in Christ." . . . I had been so blinded by an ideology that divided people by skin color that I missed the blessing of seeing the sufficiency of Christ's atonement.[15]

Such deconstruction from stifling social-justice ideologies is common, albeit underreported.[16] If you think by abandoning historic Christianity for today's trending Social Justice B ideologies you'll somehow find freedom from hard-hearted hypocrisy, I encourage you to listen carefully to such deconversion stories. Dogmatism, exclusion, and self-righteousness aren't just church problems; they're human problems.

QUESTION 4: AS I SEEK SOCIAL JUSTICE, AM I REPLACING THE FRUIT OF THE SPIRIT WITH RESENTMENT, SELF-RIGHTEOUSNESS, AND RAGE?

The pursuit of real justice bears righteous fruit; counterfeit justice does not. Is your pursuit of justice bearing love, joy, peace, patience, kindness, and the other fruits of the Holy Spirit, or is it fostering

14. "Monique's Story" in *Confronting Injustice without Compromising Truth*, 107–8.
15. "Edwin's Story" in *Confronting Injustice without Compromising Truth*, 51–52.
16. I highly recommend Alisa Childers's story in *Another Gospel? A Lifelong Christian Seeks Truth in Response to Progressive Christianity* (Carol Stream, IL: Tyndale Momentum, 2020).

rotten fruit? Are you filled with more or less suspicion, anxiety, and bitterness? Do you assume bigotry, hate, and ignorance are the best or only explanations for why others disagree with you?[17] Do you love the unique image-bearers of God before you, or do you indulge in prejudice based on skin tone, gender, or status? As one ex-Social Justice B proponent reflected, "I did not engage with individuals as individuals, but as porcelain, always thinking first and foremost of the group identities we inhabited." It left him "exhausted and misanthropic."[18] Ramirez again says it better than I can:

> What effect is reading oppression into virtually all of life having on your soul? What do you see first when you encounter a fellow Christian, their "in Christ" identity as your brother or sister or whether their appearance places them in the oppressed or oppressor group? . . . I know from experience how a noble desire for justice can replace love in our hearts with resentment and hate. I know because it happened to me. But by God's grace, and God's grace alone, I have been set free. I pray that you too can exchange suspicion and rage . . . for the love and joy of the gospel of Christ.[19]

QUESTION 5: AS I SEEK SOCIAL JUSTICE, AM I HEEDING THE GRANDFATHERLY WISDOM OF JOHN PERKINS?

John Perkins is one of my heroes, a living legend of the civil-rights movement whom I'm proud to call brother, mentor, and even friend. He is a champion of Social Justice A. His life embodies how you can pursue justice for 60-plus years without compromising the gospel one inch. I leave you with his four admonitions to the next generation of justice-seekers:

17. As Thomas Schreiner warns, "Beware of charging that someone is outside the bounds of orthodoxy when in fact the only issue is that they disagree with you." Thomas Schreiner, "Beware Theological Dangers on Both Left and Right," The Gospel Coalition, August 18, 2018, www.thegospelcoalition.org/article/orthodoxy-dangers-left-right.
18. Conor Barnes, "Sad Radicals," Quillette, December 11, 2018, https://quillette.com/2018/12/11/sad-radicals.
19. "Edwin's Story" in *Confronting Injustice without Compromising Truth*, 52.

First, *start with God!* . . . If we don't start with him first, whatever we're seeking, it ain't justice. Second, *be one in Christ!* Christian brothers and sisters—black, white, brown, rich, and poor—we are family. . . . If we give a foothold to any kind of tribalism that could tear down that unity, then we aren't bringing God's justice. Third, *preach the gospel!* The gospel of Jesus's incarnation, his perfect life, his death as our substitute, and his triumph over sin and death is good news for everyone. . . . If we replace the gospel with this or that man-made political agenda, then we ain't doing biblical justice. Fourth and finally, *teach truth!* Without truth, there can be no justice. And what is the ultimate standard of truth? It is not our feelings. It is not popular opinion. It is not what presidents or politicians say. God's Word is the standard of truth. If we're trying harder to align with the rising opinions of our day than with the Bible, then we ain't doing real justice.[20]

Your deepest longings for justice can only be satisfied within a deep and rich Christian faith. Don't give up your pursuit of justice; in fact, take it further. Re-envision your breakup as a breakthrough. Instead of bailing on the church, stick around and work to show how beautiful and compelling justice can be when we start with God, championing unity, proclaiming the gospel of historic Christianity, and following his Word as the standard of truth.

20.   John Perkins, foreword, *Confronting Injustice without Compromising Truth*, xv–xvi.

10

SCIENCE: WHY SCIENTISM CAN'T EXPLAIN MORALITY OR REALITY

KEITH PLUMMER

Every semester I require students in my Christian apologetics classes to interview a non-Christian using questions I've prepared. I don't want them to start a debate with the person; I just want them to become more comfortable asking questions of people who don't share their beliefs, to practice the skill of listening, and to better understand non-Christian thought.

This is one set of the questions: "Is there anything that could persuade you that Christianity is true? If so, what? If not, why?" My students commonly hear requests for empirical or sensory evidence. Some describe this as needing "tangible" evidence, while others speak of needing "scientific" proof for the existence of God or the possibility of miracles.

In either case, people seem to assume that only what can be scientifically confirmed is worth being called "evidence." Maybe that's your assumption, too, and a reason why you're deconstructing your faith. If so, I think you're asking the impossible of science.

Science is a wonderful means of discovering the workings of the natural world. But claiming reality is restricted only to that which we're capable of detecting with our senses is, as philosopher Alvin Plantinga has said, like a drunk looking for his lost car keys under a streetlight because the light is better there. It's a form of naturalism or materialism, a view that holds that the natural world is all that exists. This claim is not scientific in nature but philosophical. It's not a scientific conclusion but an ideological pre-commitment concerning the nature of reality.

PROBLEM OF SCIENTISM

The demand that God's existence be subject to scientific verification fails to account for the kind of being Christianity claims he is. It's to treat God as if he is simply a part of creation rather than the one who, according to the Bible, is responsible for not only creating all that is not himself but also maintaining its existence. As the apostle Paul proclaimed to the philosophers of Athens, he is the "Lord of heaven and earth" who "made the world and everything in it" (Acts 17:24). Because all creation owes its original and continued existence to God, we shouldn't expect him to be detectable as if he were simply a grander piece of nature's furniture. He qualitatively transcends what he has made; he's not a part of it. Saying you can only believe that the God of the Bible is there if empirical science confirms it is essentially to say that you'll only believe Christianity is true if it's other than what it is.

Not only does the demand for scientific or empirical evidence fail to recognize the limits of science, it artificially restricts the meaning of evidence. I'm not willing to concede the absence of scientific findings consistent with and supportive of a Christian perspective. But, for the sake of argument, the biblical narrative still makes sense of existential phenomena common to humanity, such as our aspirations for justice, our belief in human rights, our appreciation of beauty, and the inevitability of making moral judgments about human behavior. These values may not be scientific, but they should still be acknowledged as evidence. They're simply other *kinds* of evidence.

The belief that science is the only way of knowing what's true or real is called "scientism." Many, even if they've never heard the word, take scientism for granted as if it's self-evident. It's so deeply ingrained in some people's minds that they regard anyone who would dare contest it as backward and anti-scientific. But that's to conflate science and scientism. One can (and, as I'll argue, should) reject scientism without disparaging science. Even aside from the evaluation of Christianity's claims, scientism is intellectually and existentially flawed. I'd like to examine just a few problems with scientism that you might not have thought about—including one major difficulty related to whether Christianity warrants your trust.

Perhaps the greatest intellectual deficit of scientism is that it's self-refuting. It fails to meet its own standard. Remember, according to scientism, science is the only way of knowing what's true or real. If something hasn't been verified by science, we're not justified in saying we know it to be true or real. We can say we *believe* it, but we can't legitimately claim to *know* it. The problem for scientism arises, though, when we ask: "How do I know that science is the only means of knowing what's true or real?" If that assertion is really true, then the only acceptable answer to that question would have to be "Science says." If we appeal to anything other than science to answer the question, we've denied its exclusive claim. But while the sentence makes a claim *about* science, it's not a scientific claim. There's no way to establish its truth on the basis of experimentation or sensory experience. That's because it's not a scientific conclusion but a philosophical commitment to a particular theory about the means to and extent of our knowledge.

But self-refutation isn't scientism's only problem. It also has high existential costs. For example, if it were really the case that science and sensory experience are the only means of arriving at true knowledge, then we would have to admit there are many things we assume we know that we actually can't know. For example, even though you might not be a historian, you probably think you have some knowledge of past events (globally, nationally, and locally). Is your knowledge of any of those things based on science or empirical confirmation? No, because historical knowledge is not the result of repeated experimentation and observation. A great deal of our knowledge of the past depends on the testimony of people who lived in those times. But if scientism were true, then we'd have to give up any claim of historical knowledge, since it wouldn't be the finding of science. Even claims to knowledge of the recent past, including ours, would have to be abandoned if science is the only means of knowing what is true or real. I have no doubt that I ate a chicken burrito bowl for lunch shortly before typing this paragraph. But my knowledge of that delicious meal doesn't rest on science. Of course, someone could pump my stomach and verify that I did, in fact, consume what I claim; that would be a finding of science. But that in no way means my confidence concerning what I ate isn't knowledge.

MORAL KNOWLEDGE

Moral knowledge is yet another casualty of scientism. When you insist that truth is restricted to scientific verifiability, you must do away with all claims concerning knowledge of right and wrong, justice and injustice, and moral obligation. Science isn't capable of detecting or determining the existence of such entities as objective moral values and duties, since they're not subject to apprehension by the senses. But are you willing for that reason to deny that they are real? To be consistent with scientism, you must.

To illustrate this point, I ask students to imagine this situation: to a willing participant, I attach a number of devices to monitor physical activity such as blood pressure, heart rate, perspiration, brain activity, and so on. Imagine I apply to the same individual, increasing electrical shocks through electrodes attached to various parts of his body. Throughout the experiment, an assistant monitors the devices tracking his vital signs. What will the assistant observe? No doubt, we'll find that as the voltage increases, there will be a corresponding increase in heart, blood pressure, and perspiration rates. We would probably hear vocalizations and cries of increasing decibels as the experiment progressed.

What could we legitimately conclude from this experiment? We could conclude that increased electrical voltage applied to a living subject results in mounting pain accompanied by a variety of observable elevations in the bodily systems we have monitored. What we could not conclude, on the basis of what was observed, is that one *ought not* inflict such pain on another. We couldn't rightfully say, in other words, that it's wrong to do so. Moral obligations simply aren't the kind of thing science can detect or quantify.

But let me ask you something. Do you *know* it's wrong to unnecessarily inflict excruciating pain on another? Do you know it's really wrong to physically or mentally abuse another person? If scientism is true, you don't and you can't. There's no third way. Either abandon scientism or your claim to know moral truths; you can't have both. If moral outrage at perceived injustice, suffering, abuse, and cruelty is to be anything more than a mere expression of personal or group preference, it must be grounded in something real, unchanging, and not of our making.

MORAL OBJECTIONS

Moral disillusionment and disappointment with Christianity might be reasons for thinking about abandoning the faith you once professed. So many of the objections to Christianity I hear lately are moral in nature. Maybe you've been seriously injured by the church or someone professing to follow Jesus. Or perhaps recent revelations about the sins and hypocrisy of highly respected Christian leaders have led you to wonder whether Christianity is true. Or perhaps as you've watched continuous coverage of suffering caused by COVID-19, racial strife, political polarization, and various forms of injustice and dehumanization, you've concluded that the God you once claimed to love probably isn't there after all. You have some sense of the way things *ought* to be but are clearly not. Deep within there's a nagging sense that life is broken. You're making inescapable moral evaluations based on what you take as real moral standards. You have a sense of moral indignation that only makes sense if, in fact, there is true right and wrong, justice and injustice. If you're clinging to scientism, you're undermining your moral objections to the faith.

C. S. Lewis, the Christian apologist who spent many years of his life as an atheist, recounts the effect this realization had on him. His argument against God had for a long time been based on the apparent injustice and cruelty of the universe. But then he asked himself a question that, if you haven't already asked it, I hope you will: "How had I got this idea of *just* and *unjust*?" He added:

> A man does not call a line crooked unless he has some idea of a straight line. What was I comparing this universe with when I called it unjust? If the whole show was bad and senseless from A to Z, so to speak, why did I, who was supposed to be part of the show, find myself in such violent reaction against it?

Lewis rightly realized that if the universe was all there was and riddled through with meaninglessness (because there is no "Meaner" behind it), then there wasn't anything to account for his opposition to the way things are. He would just be another part of the meaningless whole. He then made a crucial point about the relationship between his argument against God and the necessity of an objective standard of justice:

> Of course I could have given up my idea of justice by saying it was nothing but a private idea of my own. But if I did that, then my argument against God collapsed too—for the argument depended on saying that the world was really unjust, not simply that it did not happen to please my private fancies.

I really dislike lima beans. (Bear with me.) I've despised them since childhood, when my mother would insist I eat them in servings of mixed vegetables. I found their consistency and flavor so distasteful that I did my best to swallow them. Decades later, if my wife serves mixed vegetables with lima beans, I try to down them as fast as possible without biting into and feeling their mushiness. What if I were to propose an argument, let's call it "the problem of lima beans," that said a good, all-powerful God can't exist because lima beans do, and I don't like them? Would you find that argument at all compelling? I hope you wouldn't. God's existence and my dislike of lima beans are unrelated. It doesn't follow that God can't exist because he has permitted things I don't prefer. It wouldn't even follow if I found a large group of others who hate lima beans. Personal and collective tastes are still subjective. My confident assertion that lima beans are nasty gives you insight into my preferences, but it doesn't really tell you anything about the nature of lima beans.

This is what Lewis was getting at when he said that his argument against God failed if his idea of justice was simply a "private idea of my own." His calling life unjust would be on the same order as my saying, "Lima beans are nasty," a mere articulation of his personal taste that didn't actually say anything about the world outside himself. In order for his evaluation that the universe was unjust to carry any weight, there had to be an actual, absolute standard of goodness and justice by which he made his assessment. This led him to conclude:

> Thus, in the very act of trying to prove that God did not exist—in other words, that the whole of reality was senseless—I found I was forced to assume that one part of reality—namely my idea of justice—was full of sense. If the whole universe has no meaning, we should never have found out that it has no meaning: just as, if there were no light in the universe and therefore no creatures with eyes, we should never have known it was dark. Dark would be without meaning.[1]

Before you conclude there is no evidence for Christianity, consider that your moral intuition bears witness to the God of the Bible. Christianity makes sense of the inevitability of making moral judgments about others and ourselves. We can try with all our might to deny it, but we can't escape on some level thinking that there is a moral straight line, *any* deviation from which is evil. I emphasized the word "any" because we tend to reserve the word "evil" for what we regard as the greatest atrocities (usually those we don't commit ourselves). But just as any deviation from a perfectly straight line constitutes crookedness, any deviation from pure goodness is evil. And that's a problem for each of us, for which only the Christian faith is the solution.

1.   C. S. Lewis, *Mere Christianity* (orig., 1952; New York: Touchstone, 1996), 46.

11

ANTI-INTELLECTUALISM: WE MUST ASK HARD QUESTIONS

KAREN SWALLOW PRIOR

"Literature is trash."

Or so a college freshman once informed me, an English professor. The student, who was majoring in one of the sciences, felt indignant about the English requirements in the university's core curriculum. If Christians have to read literature, he said, the literature should be explicitly Christian. Even the best classics are "a waste of time," he complained. Shakespeare might be clever, but he's not edifying.

Opinions like his weren't new to me. But I had seldom encountered them in someone so young and so certain. And in college. When I shared with him a biblical basis for studying and enjoying literature, he responded by pontificating on the doctrines of presuppositionalism, on the failures of Paul's approach to apologetics at Mars Hill, on the glories of the pure gospel untainted by worldly imaginations. It seemed like a hopeless case.

Within a few years, he had renounced his faith.

Now he has found his place among fellow atheistic young scholars expressing hostility and disdain toward religious belief, especially Christianity. I asked him once how this deconstruction had happened. He said that encountering ideas he'd never been exposed to before led him to reconsider everything he'd been taught, particularly some claims by Christians in his area of study that he now considers fabrications.

Although such a dramatic turnabout surprised me at first, the more I reflected on it the more I understood it might've been expected. I wish I could say that his trajectory—from earnest, unquestioning believer to cynical, incredulous skeptic—was unusual. But after more than two decades of teaching college students in an evangelical context, I know, sadly, that it's not.

People abandon their faith for various reasons, of course. But in my particular context—teaching Christian young people in Christian institutions—the stumbling block I encounter most often is anti-intellectualism.

THE PROBLEM

Anti-intellectualism has a fairly specific meaning. It isn't merely being opposed to the use of the intellect; rather, it opposes intellectualism, which places the intellect above all else. Intellectualism emerged in the modern age by placing reason above all other sources of knowledge. Anti-intellectualism is an equal and opposite reaction against this shift, as seen in the way Dictionary.com defines it as opposition to "intellectuals and the modern academic, artistic, social, religious, and other theories associated with them." It's human nature to react to one extreme by swinging to the opposite extreme, to exchange one form of fundamentalism for another. But often truth and virtue reside in the balance, and anti-intellectualism creates a kind of all-or-nothing approach that ultimately fails.

The staging ground for many seemingly unresolvable tensions between faith and reason is often science (as was the case with my former student). This makes sense given science's defining role in modernity. The beginnings of modernity were deeply tied to Christian thought. For centuries, many of the most revolutionary and groundbreaking scientific discoveries were made by those who adhered to the Christian faith, and the church actively supported the advance of such knowledge.[1] But eventually, particularly in the 19th century with the rise of Darwinism and higher criticism, the church simply failed to compete with scientific theories that posed increasing challenges to Christian belief.

The word "science" comes from the Latin word for "knowledge." It's significant that the word now used to refer to the study of the physical, material world originally referred to all types of knowledge. This conflation is quite telling: it suggests a worldview in which all knowledge is the *scientific* kind, leaving no room for things like emotional intelligence, intuition, or supernatural revelation.

However, entering what some call the postmodern age, rejection of modernity's rigid, scientific categories became more common. While this new paradigm carries risks, it also opens up the possibility for a more holistic understanding that sees reason and faith as less opposed than once thought. Many younger Christians are being discipled within the framework of a Christian worldview, taught to integrate of all aspects of life into a biblical framework, and they're bearing good fruit: resisting attempts to cordon off any area of life from another, asking questions, seeking understanding, and striving for logical coherence that many of our modern categories lack.

The church needs this course correction.

Yet, still largely shaped by the modernist battles, many churches today lag behind these younger believers. The ancient creeds, confessions, and doctrines that define the church universal have not and cannot change. But the application of these truths within any particular human culture will inevitably reflect the qualities and quirks of their age.

---

1.   See, for example, Stephen M. Barr, *Modern Physics and Ancient Faith* (Notre Dame, IN: University of Notre Dame), 2006.

WE NEED THEOLOGICAL TRIAGE

This is one reason theologians throughout history have "drawn a distinction between essential and non-essential beliefs," as Gavin Ortlund explains.[2] Failing to differentiate among first-tier, second-tier, and third-tier doctrines, writes Randall Rauser, encourages believers to mistake "an interpretation of Christianity for Christianity itself." When an "excessive number of doctrines and practices" rise "to the level of the non-negotiable," this creates "a house of cards faith," and if any one doctrine is rejected, "the entire edifice will collapse."[3]

Erica Carlson, a Christian physics professor at Purdue University, says this lack of a theological triage creates a "glass theology." Like a car made of glass that has no shock absorbers, such a faith shatters upon hitting any bump in the road. This phenomenon is particularly common among Christian young people who arrive at college ill-equipped to reconcile the competing truth claims of Christianity and academia. As a result, they feel compelled to choose between them. But when Christians hold theological beliefs within a hierarchy that assigns core doctrines a higher value than secondary doctrines, that core is less likely to be abandoned when the non-essentials encounter friction.[4]

HUNGER FOR ANSWERS

The young Christians I know today don't want a "glass theology" or a "house of cards faith." They hunger for deep, robust faith. In fact, overprotectiveness, shallowness, and anti-science attitude are high among the characteristics of the church that have pushed young people away.[5] Many younger Christians in one study reported feeling that "they

2.   Gavin Ortlund. *Finding the Right Hills to Die on: The Case for Theological Triage* (Wheaton, IL: Crossway, 2020), 29.

3.   Randall Rauser, "The Problem of Christians Becoming Atheists," The Christian Post, December 21, 2018, https://www.christianpost.com/voices/the-problem-of-christians-becoming-atheists.html.

4.   Erica Carlson, "Can I Ask That in Church?," Southeastern Baptist Theological Seminary, https://www.youtube.com/watch?v=kBA9YTWnFVA.

5.   David Kinnaman, "Why Young Christians Are Leaving the Church . . . and Rethinking Faith," *In Part*, http://www.inpart.org/feature/you-lost-me.

have been offered slick or half-baked answers to their thorny, honest questions, and they are rejecting the 'talking heads' or 'talking point'" approach common in their experience.[6] I hear stories like this from frustrated young Christians over and over.

One told me of her experience growing up in church: "I feel like my brain was on forced snooze for nearly 40 years." Another bitterly recalls a senior pastor who said that studying Greek and Hebrew isn't helpful to studying the Bible and that using Bible commentaries can impede the work of the Holy Spirit. Another younger Christian was warned by fellow church members that her decision to attend seminary would cause her to lose her "simple faith." The parents of a young professor I know so disbelieve in higher education that, although their son remains a Christian and teaches at a Christian college, they perceive him distrustfully as part of a larger, liberalizing force that only corrupts the faithful. My friend endures his parents' quiet disapproval as a deep, painful, and unnecessary rift that remains beyond human repair. Christian artists can especially feel lonely in the church. The sense that their gifts are being rejected too often leads to their leaving. Even Christians who enjoy rather than create art are often discouraged by the poor quality and cheap messages of Christian popular culture. And this problem is more than a matter of mere taste. As Dorothy Sayers pointedly wrote of "shoddy, weak, sentimental religious art":

> [T]here are pious souls who get comfort out of bad stained glass and sloppy hymns and music (though they might well have got better nourishment out of honest stuff). But thousands of others have spewed at the sight and sound of it, and said "If Christianity fosters that kind of thing it must have a lie in its soul."[7]

MY STORY

Growing up in the church, I didn't see my love of books, especially those that challenged any kind of conventional thinking, as having

---

6. Kinnaman, "Why Young Christians Are Leaving the Church . . . and Rethinking Faith."
7. Quoted in Gina Dalfonzo, *Dorothy and Jack: The Transforming Friendship of Dorothy L. Sayers and C. S. Lewis* (Grand Rapids, MI: Baker Books, 2020), 75.

a place in the life of a Christian. Like many others, I thought I had to choose between the life of the mind and my love for God. So for a while I chose the mind. I never really doubted God or the core of Christian belief; I just didn't know how to fit them together, since I wasn't given a model for doing so.

Ironically—and sadly—it took an unbelieving professor at my secular university to show me the deep, rich tradition of Christian thinkers that is our heritage. It started with a discussion of a treatise by the 17th-century poet John Milton, who laid the foundation for modern-day concepts of free speech and freedom of the press. Many other writers we covered in my classes (in which I was the only Christian, as far as I knew) were also serious Christians: Miguel de Cervantes, Daniel Defoe, Alexander Pope, Jonathan Swift, Samuel Richardson, Mary Rowlandson, Jane Austen, William Wordsworth, Samuel Taylor Coleridge, Charlotte Brontë, Charles Dickens, and T. S. Eliot. These were believers—and there are many more beyond my limited field of expertise—whose words shaped the world and whom countless scholars continue to research and write about today.

As I later expanded my studies to aesthetics and philosophy, I discovered a trove of brilliant Christian minds assigned significant weight within the academic community: Augustine of Hippo, Francis Bacon, Desiderius Erasmus, Blaise Pascal, John Locke, Frederick Douglass, Søren Kierkegaard, Ludwig Wittgenstein, and Simone Weil, to name just a few.

And then there are the artists, inventors, and innovators (the "creatives," we might say) found throughout history and today: Johannes Gutenberg, Leonardo da Vinci, J. S. Bach, René Descartes, Robert Boyle, Isaac Newton, Johann Wolfgang von Goethe, Wolfgang Amadeus Mozart, Gregor Mendel, George Washington Carver, Vincent Van Gogh, Graham Greene, Shusaku Endo, Marilynne Robinson, Toni Morrison, Francis Collins, and Makoto Fujimura.

In encountering all these, I came to see that my understanding of the intellectual Christian tradition was narrow, limited as it was to my experience. The 2,000-year-old intellectual tradition of the church is, in fact, deep and broad, rich and glorious. By basing my understanding on little more than my experience, I was, ironically, guilty of the same narrowness of mind I was accusing others of.

HUMBLE QUESTIONING

Certainly, a long strand of anti-intellectualism is woven throughout the Christian tradition—from the mysticism of the anonymous medieval work *The Cloud of Unknowing* to the separatism adopted by many American fundamentalists in the 20th century to the widespread embrace of conspiracy theories by many Christians today. Even so, anti-intellectualism among Christians isn't just a problem in churches; it's a problem within contemporary America. As far back as 1963, Richard Hofstadter's *Anti-Intellectualism in American Life* was deemed so significant that it won the Pulitzer Prize.[8] More recently, Tom Nichols's *The Death of Expertise* examines today's rampant anti-intellectualism throughout our society in the form of growing hostility toward the authority of experts.[9] Nichols attributes this phenomenon, paradoxically, to our higher educational attainments and wider access to information and knowledge. In other words, armed with a little education and a little information, we're often apt to place more confidence in our less-informed opinions than in the knowledge of those with expertise. Like the proverbial sophomore (literally, a "wise fool"), we prove the words of the eighteenth century poet Alexander Pope when he mused, "A little knowledge is a dangerous thing."

The way of virtue—in matters of intellect, as in all things—is to avoid both the extreme of deficiency and the extreme of excess. It's good for those of us granted the ability and opportunity to pursue the life of the mind to steward that gift well and to encourage others to do the same, without disdain for those with less education or opportunity. Intellectual pursuit apart from intellectual humility is fruitless.

ASK HARD QUESTIONS

In his ministry on earth, Jesus loved hard questions. He welcomed them from others, and he asked them himself. He commanded his followers to "love the Lord your God with all your heart and with

8.   Richard Hofstadter, *Anti-Intellectualism in American Life* (New York: Knopf, 1963).
9.   Tom Nichols, *The Death of Expertise: The Campaign against Established Knowledge and Why It Matters* (New York: Oxford University Press, 2017).

all your soul and with all your *mind*" (Matt. 22:37). In fact, in all four Gospels, Jesus assesses his disciples' faith in him through one pointed question: "Who do you say I am?"

The proper response to anti-intellectual Christianity isn't hyper-cerebral Christianity; it's cultivating an environment where skeptics are welcome, doubts are taken seriously, and we "have mercy on those who doubt" (Jude 1:22). The right questions asked in the right way can only lead to truth—and the Truth.

Before you deconstruct your faith, know that there is no question too hard for Christianity. Of course, it's one thing to affirm this theologically but another to embody this in daily church life. Our churches must be the places that welcome the questions—and those who ask them. You—with your questions and believing doubt—might be the one to help them be such a church.

12

HELL: SKELETON IN GOD'S CLOSET?

JOSHUA RYAN BUTLER

"So you think I'm going to hell?" My college roommate was interrogating me. I hadn't even mentioned hell. I was a new Christian and had simply mentioned my recent experience of Jesus and the goodness of God. But as for many today, hell was a stumbling block to his believing God could really be good.

Perhaps you've wrestled with this question, too. I know I have.

Hell used to seem to me like a skeleton in God's closet, a tough topic that—if I really opened the door of Scripture to take a closer look—would only reveal God as a cruel, vindictive tyrant. You might even be considering walking away from the faith because of this topic.

Before you go, however, I want to offer a few paradigm shifts that have helped me over the years. I've found many of us have a caricature of what the Bible teaches and robust Christian orthodoxy has historically proclaimed. My hope is to help you reclaim a greater confidence in the goodness of God—not in spite of this topic, but even because of it—and a deeper confidence that God is good, all the way down, in his very bones.

RECONCILING HEAVEN AND EARTH

God is on a mission to reconcile heaven and earth. This is the first paradigm shift. It has to do with the storyline hell fits into. I once had (as you might have) what I like to call the "up/down" storyline: *good folks go up, bad folks go down.* Heaven was a puffy place in the clouds where we'll play harps with angels for eternity, while hell was an underground torture chamber where little devils poke you with fiery pitchforks.

One of the many problems with this story is that there is no story: it's simply about personal reward or retribution, nothing more. It tells us nothing about how judgment (the scary side of the coin) is related to restoration (the good thing God is up to in the world). Yet in the Bible, because God is out to reconcile heaven and earth, he opposes the destructive power of hell.

Heaven's primary counterpart isn't hell in the Bible; it's earth. For example, "heaven and earth" appear together in the same verse more than 200 times in the biblical story, like a narrative thread woven throughout the Scriptures as a whole. By contrast, "heaven and hell" never appear together in the same verse. They certainly relate to each other, but the Bible has a different way of framing their relationship.

If you're deconstructing hell, first consider this: we get hell wrong, I'd suggest, because we get heaven and earth wrong. And if we reclaim the biblical story of heaven and earth, the smaller subtopic of hell will start to make more sense.

What is this story? Heaven and earth are created good by God (see Gen. 1–2), yet then torn apart by the destructive power of sin (see Gen. 3 onward). We live amid God's good world corrupted by the fall. How does God respond, however? Not ultimately by whisking us away to heaven ("Beam me up, Scotty"). Rather, the Bible is the story of God's rescue mission, to restore humanity and redeem creation.

God's mission to reconcile heaven and earth climaxes in the cross and resurrection of Christ. Check out the way the apostle Paul puts it:

> God was pleased to have all his fullness dwell in [Jesus], and through him to reconcile to himself all things, whether things on earth or things in heaven, by making peace through his blood, shed on the cross. (Col. 1:19–20, NIV)

Jesus reconciles heaven and earth. The Savior brings back together what hell has torn apart. The gospel says more than this, but definitely not less. Paul says this is what Christ accomplished on the cross.

Jesus "deconstructs" hell's dominion on the earth.

"All authority in heaven and on earth has been given to me" (Matt. 28:18), the resurrected Christ tells his disciples. Why has the Father entrusted his Son with this all-encompassing authority? In order, we're told in Ephesians, to "bring all things in *heaven* and on *earth* together under one head, even Christ" (Eph. 1:10). In the wedding feast at the end of the biblical story, in Revelation 21–22, God unites heaven and earth together forever as one.

"So what does this have to do with hell?" you might ask. Here the logic of hell starts to make sense. To long for the dawning of the light is, by its nature, to long for casting out darkness. To hope for the healing of the body is implicitly to hope for excising the disease. To pray with Jesus, "Your kingdom come, your will be done, on earth as it is in heaven" (Matt. 6:10), is to pray that all those powers that stand unrepentantly opposed to God's kingdom be sent packing.

Heaven breaking into earth means pushing hell out. There is a symmetry between hope for the coming of God's kingdom and hope for Christ's judgment on unrepentant sin that unleashes havoc in our world. Deliverance from the destructive power of sin, death, and hell makes it possible to finally reconcile heaven and earth.

Because God is good, he is on a mission to reconcile heaven and earth. Or we can say the same thing from another angle: God is on a mission to get the hell out of earth.

GETTING THE HELL OUT OF EARTH

God's mission isn't to get *us* the hell out of earth (an escapist story), but to get the hell *out of us* on earth (a redemptive story). This is the second paradigm shift. You might be deconstructing a vindictive God with a chip on his shoulder, but in the gospel we're the ones who've unleashed hell's destructive power in the world, seen on massive systemic levels like sex-trafficking and genocide, and on intimate personal levels like pride, lust, rage, and greed—things we all struggle with. We've truly brought hell on earth.

Jesus says the vices of the human heart are the sparks that set the world aflame. He relates our corrupted affections—like lust and rage—to the reality of hell (Matt. 5:21–27). The problem isn't only "out there" but "in here," Jesus insists, within each of us. The heart of the problem is the problem of the heart.

Fire imagery is used many ways in Scripture, but one way is to speak to the destructive power of sin. For example, "Consider what a great forest is set on fire by a small spark. The tongue also is a fire . . . it corrupts the whole body, sets the whole course of one's life on fire, and is itself set on fire by hell" (James 3:5–6).

All it takes is a spark from your campfire to burn down Redwood National Park. Similarly, your tongue is small, but its words can wreak havoc, burning down your life and community. And when it does, notice where James says the tongue's power comes from: it is "set on fire by hell."

This should be shocking: hell's wildfire power is unleashed into the world through us.

Fire is an apt image for hell's destructive power. It doesn't build things up; it burns them down. When your colleague gossips in the adjacent cubicle, this passage suggests, she's not just being annoying, she's *breathing hell* into the office, tearing people down with her words. If wicked words can do this, how much more so the broader works of evil in our lives?

Hell deconstructs God's good world.

Yet because of God's great compassion, he doesn't leave us to ourselves. God showers the waters of his extravagant mercy on the sin-scorched humanity he's brought up from the dust. On the cross, Jesus bore the wildfire of our wickedness, to exhaust its force and extinguish its flame, and offer us union with him.

As we stand before Jesus, his question isn't "Are you good enough to get into my kingdom?" but "Will you let me heal you?"

When we're united with Jesus, we become a place where heaven and earth are reconciled—and hell is pushed out. "That's beautiful," you might say, "but what about those who refuse the King's mercy?" Where does hell's power go when sin is banished from his kingdom? We've discussed the *story* of hell and the *origin* of its power in the world; let's turn now to the *location* of hell.

OUTSIDE THE CITY

You might envision hell as an "underground torture chamber." But Jesus says its location is "outside the city." The dominant New Testament word translated into English as "hell" is *Gehenna*. It might surprise you to know this was an actual physical place, just outside the walls of Jerusalem (you can find it on Google Maps). This was a place you could walk to.

Gehenna had a dark and dangerous history. In the Old Testament, it's known as the Valley of Hinnom, and its primary association is with child sacrifice (for some gruesome examples, read 2 Chron. 28:1–4 and 33:3–9). Here Israel slaughtered her children in worship of other gods. God was incensed at the practice, crying out, "Never did I command such a thing!" (Jer. 32:35).

For the prophets, the notorious valley became a symbol of Israel's idolatry and injustice. Yet the prophets hoped that one day, God would return as King to reclaim Jerusalem as his capital and establish his kingdom of justice. When he did, God would kick all the impenitent rebels and destructive powers outside his city, into, yes, the Valley of Hinnom.

There's a logic here. The reason hell's destructive power is kicked *outside* the city is that it opposes the good and redemptive things God wants to do *inside* the city. To ask for God's kingdom to come and hell to stick around is like asking the doctor to heal your body but leave the cancer, like asking for restoration to come and destruction to remain. It's to ask for a contradiction.

God excludes sin from his kingdom *because of* his goodness, not in opposition to or in spite of it. As you're tempted to deconstruct, you might consider what it is you're actually asking God to do, if you truly want him to heal the world.

You might also find it interesting that the flames in *Gehenna* were lit by human hands. This fact provides an interesting backdrop for the fire imagery. The people killing their children were returning to the city to sleep at night; the idols they sacrificed to were soon set up in the temple (see 2 Chron. 33:1–9). So God's judgment here pushes the rebellion back to where it came from, and involves a sense of "You made your bed, now lie in it."

God is active in judgment, but an aspect of his judgment is handing us over to what we've chosen. God sets himself against the arsonists who burn up his world.

So hell's location isn't underground; it's outside the city. You also see this picture in the new Jerusalem of Revelation 21, at the end of the biblical story, when evil is kept outside and not allowed to enter God's city (v. 27). Our future hope isn't "Good folks go up, bad folks go down," but this: God will re-establish his good kingdom at the center of the world, while evil and all its allies are banished to the periphery. It's a "center/periphery" story.

You might wonder what this means for God's *purpose* in judgment. Let's turn to that now.

PROTECTING THE KINGDOM

God's purpose is protection. He's out to safeguard his beloved. "They shall not hurt or destroy in all my holy mountain," he says in Isaiah 11:9 of his kingdom coming to Mount Zion (Jerusalem). When Jesus returns, all those forces who harm and destroy today will finally be kept at bay. Similarly, in Zechariah 2:4–5, God says of his coming kingdom: "'Jerusalem will be a city without walls because of the great number of people and animals in it. And I myself will be a wall of fire around it,' declares the LORD, 'and I will be its glory within.'"

That's a powerful image: God wants people in his city so strongly—wants *you* in his city so strongly—he tears down the walls to make room for the masses, letting all who will receive him come in. If you were an ancient Israelite, however, this welcome posed a problem. *What about our enemies, God? The walls protect us from hostile invasion.* God answers, declaring he himself will be its protection. "I myself will be a wall of fire around it."

God protects his city not with tanks, jet fighters, and AK-47s.

God protects his city with his very presence.

I find it interesting that God's presence is experienced *inside* the city as redemptive glory and *outside* the city as protective fire. Same presence; different purpose. God is always light, life, and love—we can't change his holy presence: his nature is immutable, his character unchanging. But the radiant beauty of God's glorious presence is exercised in judgment upon those who cling to darkness and death, who harden their hearts against him and his ways, in a posture of unrepentant sin.

So don't harden your heart.

Perhaps you've envisioned hell as a "chamber," where people are crying out to God in repentance, "I'm sorry! I love you. I'll do anything to be with you." In a strange reversal of the gospel, we're the ones pursuing God while he refuses to be found. This is backward. In the gospel, God has pursued us in Christ, going all the way to hell and back to be with us. Our deeper issue is the problem of the hardened heart. This cardiovascular image speaks to our rejection of God, not just with a few bad acts but with a disposition that desires distance from him, preferring autonomy to worship, independence to communion, our sin to his salvation.

Our problem isn't that God is cold-hearted, but that we are hard-hearted.

This is what some have meant in saying, "The doors of hell are locked from the inside." It's not to say God is sitting by while we go our own way: he actively identifies, judges, and deals appropriately with our sin. It's also not to say we have a "second chance" on the other side of the grave: being hard-hearted means your answer would be the same. But it is to say God's judgment aligns—it fits—with our rebellion. God does not lock the bolt against our *repentant* will, but rather through our *unrepentant* will. When we reject God, preferring the darkness of our self-enclosed existence to the expansive and liberating light of his, we become the skeletons in God's closet.

Our desire for freedom from God gives rise to our slavery to sin. Sin is the root; hell is the fruit.

HELL-DEFEATING SAVIOR

Jesus is a hell-defeating, fire-extinguishing, life-giving King. The good news of the gospel is that the Savior invites us into his city. The King loves to pardon. The Lamb desires to forgive. The Great Physician rejoices to heal. On the cross, Jesus opens his arms wide to embrace our sin-struck, war-torn world—and absorb the wildfire we've unleashed. Though we're rebels, his voice calls us "Daughter" and "Son." He raises his voice strong and calls to the ends of the earth, beckoning us to receive his reconciling presence and prepare for the resurrection to come.

Don't let your deconstruction drive you from Jesus, for his might alone can deconstruct the power of hell in your life; his Spirit alone can soften your hardened heart; his grace alone can restore you with the goodness of God. Throw away the caricatures, yes, but through union with Christ you can become a place where heaven and earth are one, and join with his people to bear witness to the kingdom to come.

Speaking of "joining with his people to bear witness," we now turn to the third and final section of this book, to explore what it looks like to reconstruct a healthy faith.

PART THREE

RECONSTRUCT
FAITH

13

EMBRACE TRUE BELONGING IN THE CHURCH

JEREMY LINNEMAN

In the 18th century, along the East Coast of the future United States as it was being colonized, two groups of people lived side by side. The first group, the indigenous people, maintained a simple way of life that had been unchanged for thousands of years. The second, the European colonists, represented the more modern society in their economy, culture, industry, and technology.

Despite little interaction between the two communities, one of them began to be interested in the other, and many individuals and families began to leave their social group to join the other. But in a surprise to modern readers, it was the British colonists leaving and joining the tribes of the indigenous people, not the other way around.

In several instances, British colonists were captured during battle by the indigenous people. But rather than being killed or imprisoned, the colonists were often integrated as members of the Native communities. When the colonists would finally rescue these individuals and return them to their colonies, the one-time captives would often seek to return to the tribes.

Benjamin Franklin wrote to a friend in 1753, "Tho' ransomed by their friends, and treated with all imaginable tenderness to prevail with them to stay among the English, yet in a short time they become disgusted with our manner of life ... and take the first good opportunity of escaping again into the woods."

Still others voluntarily left British society to join the tribes of the Natives. They walked into the woods and never looked back. After some time, the frontier tribes were full of white men who had left behind their people and culture, married Native women, and made a home for themselves.

French historian Hector de Crèvecoeur tried to make sense of it all in 1782. "Thousands of Europeans are Indians, and we have no examples of even one of those Aborigines having from choice become European. There must be in their social bond something singularly captivating and far superior to anything to be boasted of among us."[1]

The seeds of radical individualism were being planted, and already the early Americans began to feel empty, disconnected, and lonely. In the Native tribes, they found something "far superior" to the economy, industry, and technology of their modern society.

What did they find? And how did they so immediately recognize it, and leaving everything behind, cling to it for the rest of their lives?

That's what this chapter is about—the tragic loss of belonging in the West, how radical individualism has "de-formed" members of American churches (weakening the faith and causing many young people to run in the other direction), and why the more relational, connected way of life we seek is available only within true, historic Christianity.

---

1.   Sebastian Junger, *Tribe: On Belonging and Homecoming* (New York: Twelve Publishing, 2016), 3.

My hope and prayer is that you might deconstruct the promises of Western secularism (which is entrenched in the emptiness of radical individualism and leads to chronic loneliness) and rediscover the hope of a rooted, interconnected life in Christ.

AMERICAN CHRISTIANITY'S 'ME' PROBLEM

I was born in May 1984, making me an elder millennial. I was raised in a large charismatic/evangelical congregation and attended a Christian private school. From my graduating class—mostly students from stable, church-attending families—my guess is that only a quarter of them are still walking with the Lord and participating in a local church about 20 years later. Including my experience with a college ministry, I suspect I've seen far more close friends leave the Christian faith and community than remain within it. Deconstruction has become more popular and mainstream than faithful spiritual life.

Why?

When I read or hear deconversion testimonies in personal conversations or on Facebook, blogs, and podcasts, one theme almost always sticks out. The deconversion script typically includes some variation of the following: "I was raised in a religious home, and we attended church (at least once) every week. But the people there were often judgmental and close-minded, while I discovered my non-Christian friends to be easygoing and affirming. My church experience was about what to believe and how to behave, but my experience with my unbelieving friends was about who I could become and how I was already enough."

So often, my friends who have deconstructed and then left the historic Christian faith have said they experienced more grace, friendship, and community somewhere other than the church—whether it was a fraternity or sorority, a social club or place of employment, or even a political party.

When they describe why they're leaving the church—they rarely use the language of deconstruction, and most never take the time to post a manifesto online—this point of belonging and community is revealing. The Christianity they experienced was a system of belief only and not a genuine faith community. This often reflects more of the individualistic Western way of life than the relational, intimate way of Jesus.

What do I mean? Some church buildings are designed to feel like shopping centers, complete with bookstores, T-shirt kiosks, and video-game theaters for teenagers. Many churches resemble American consumerism in their message, too: "Believe in Jesus, and he will make you successful." Meanwhile, much New Testament Christianity is often lacking—including service to the poor and needy, vibrant hospitable community, and life-giving pastoral care.

The form of Christianity they have left is a form of religion that I want to leave as well.

Indeed, much of American Christianity has drifted from this essential aspect of historic Christian life. Historic Christianity teaches that we're relational beings—created in the image of a triune God (Father, Son, and Holy Spirit) who has eternally existed in relationship. But much of American Christianity has flowed with mainstream culture in promoting personal autonomy, rugged individualism, and consumer culture. Historic Christianity teaches that true belonging is found in being fully known and fully loved by God and others. Yet American Christianity often follows secularism's vision of the good life through production and consumption.

If your experience of Christianity has been largely individualistic ("just Jesus and me"), or if you've had a primarily frustrating experience among believers, this chapter is for you. I want you to deconstruct this individualist form of Christianity, and to rediscover the beauty of spiritual community in Christ.

DECONSTRUCTING INDIVIDUALISM

What's so wrong with the individualist worldview? Three things, at least.

1. THE INDIVIDUALIST WORLDVIEW FAILS TO RECOGNIZE OUR NATURE AS HUMAN

Sure, Christian theology teaches that we are relational beings because we are made in the image of a relational God. But this point is also echoed in neuroscience, social psychology, and even sports. Functional MRI scans (brain imaging conducted in real time as a person responds to various stimuli) show that loneliness affects the brain in a profound way.[2] Social psychologists have discovered over decades-long studies that having "a place to belong" relates to well-being more than any other factor does.[3]

2. THE INDIVIDUALIST WORLDVIEW CAUSES OUR RELATIONSHIPS TO BE HOLLOW AND SHALLOW

Living from the mindset of the individual (as opposed to the interconnected person-in-community) will mean that relationships become transactional. They become a function of what we can give and take from each other. We are no longer fully known, and we certainly aren't fully loved; instead we give and receive help to further our individualist pursuits—whether career, education, or otherwise. Transactional relationships are, by definition, hollow (lacking true love and commitment) and shallow (unable to learn, grow, adapt, forgive, and enjoy).

3. THE INDIVIDUALIST WORLDVIEW LIMITS OUR WELL-BEING AND FLOURISHING

When Jesus began his earthly ministry, some of his earliest and most important teaching focused on human flourishing. Recorded in Matthew 5–7, his Sermon on the Mount describes a person who is truly blessed, happy, thriving, or flourishing. Jesus then shocks us with the characteristics of such a blessed life. The blessed are not those who have earned or accumulated the most power, wealth, comfort, pleasure, or security. The truly blessed are characterized by their relationships and the quality of their character. "Blessed are the poor in spirit. . . . Blessed are the merciful. . . . Blessed are the peacemakers" (Matt. 5:3–8). In other words, "whoever would save his life will lose it, but whoever loses his life for my sake will find it" (Matt. 16:25). Radical in-

2. John T. Cacioppo, *Loneliness: Human Nature and the Need for Social Connection* (W. W. Norton & Company, 2009).

3. Roy F. Baumeister and Mark R. Leary, "The Need to Belong: Desire for Interpersonal Attachments as a Fundamental Human Motivation," *Psychological Bulletin* 117, no. 3 (May 1995): 497–529.

dividualism might enable momentary comfort and pleasure, but only true belonging will enable eternal connection and community.

HURT AND HEALING IN CHRISTIAN COMMUNITY

Many of my close friends who've left the church have suffered real disappointment and hurt at the hands of Christians. Some have suffered tragic spiritual abuse from ministry leaders. It's no surprise, then, that they've moved away from Christian community. What an awful and tragic experience! I mourn and grieve for anyone who has searched for God and family, only to find judgment, condemnation, and abuse. Lord, help us.

Much of my pastoral ministry involves caring for and rehabilitating those who have suffered church hurt. I've discovered that *we're hurt in relationship, and we find healing in relationship.*

When we're sinned against by others, the natural tendency is to move away from everyone else. When we ourselves sin and are shamed by others, it's similarly natural to withdraw into ourselves. But while this withdrawal may be a natural survival instinct, it won't lead to complete healing. At some point, we must move toward others to find comfort and healing.

If you're a child of God and have been called and commissioned to live for him with purpose, dignity, and giftedness, don't let those who have sinned against you determine your future. You may need to invest in wise counseling and spiritual direction. And from your pain, a new and deeper version of yourself can emerge. You can move toward others with trust and hope again, not because your next community won't fail you, but because God will never fail you, and he often ministers to us through others.

We're hurt in relationship, and we find healing in relationship. Before you move fully and finally away from the church, consider if you might never find what your soul truly needs until you move toward healthy, loving Christian friends and spiritual community again—or for the first time.

REDISCOVERING SPIRITUAL COMMUNITY

The good news is that spiritual community is possible. True belonging can be found. And God loves you enough to use your pain to bring about much good both in your life and in the lives of those around you.

What does it look like to rediscover Christian community—as someone who is considering leaving the faith or the church?

1. WE MUST LEARN THAT CHRISTIAN COMMUNITY IS BUILT, NOT FOUND

One of my pastor friends has often told his church, "This isn't a great place to find community—it's a great place to build community." In other words, if you're looking for a community that will welcome you into its club of happy, non-dramatic, non-demanding friends, good luck. Maybe you do find a group that says, "Come on in; it's perfect in here. We've been waiting just for you. We have everything taken care of." But that's either a false promise or it's a cult—or maybe just an overeager group workout class. No, Christian community must be built, not found.

Christian community is hard because people are hard (yes, that includes you). But it's worthwhile. And in my experience, the more time and energy you invest in helping others feel connected, the more you tend to feel connected. If you work to make a place for others, you'll likely always have a place yourself. If you're willing to take initiative, build relationships, and care for others even when it's boring, repetitive, or messy—and if you can expect this journey to count by years and not months—you will find yourself in a true and living community (Rom. 12:9–21).

2. WE MUST RESET OUR LIVES FOR RELATIONSHIPS

If community is built and not found, then we need to reset some aspects of our lives. We have to slow down and resist the culture of hurry around us. We may not be able to work late into the evening or on weekends. We need to plan ahead with the tenacity of a project manager to make a weekly small group or Bible study fit and remain in our schedules. We will need to recognize that moving every few years will significantly damage our relational connectedness and sense of belonging. A deep, connected life with others requires a new set of priorities and a new set of life rhythms. But it is so worthwhile.

3. WE MUST BE WILLING TO BE HONEST AND VULNERABLE

If you're deconstructing the faith, have you discussed it with those around you? More often than not, my friends who have left the faith (or simply their local church, while not joining another) have never shared their frustrations and concerns with their communities or leaders. Instead, others don't hear of these struggles except through Facebook, Twitter, or Medium.

But if you want others to be more honest and vulnerable with you, then you may have to begin by being more honest and vulnerable with them. If they don't respond well, don't be too discouraged. Perhaps they've never really considered the foundations of Christianity and feel threatened. Perhaps their identity is so wrapped up in a tradition or group that they can't imagine critiquing it. But in the long run, being honest and vulnerable with others will lead to deeper relationships—and if not in one community, then in another.

I'M DECONSTRUCTING

If you've left the faith and found community in a social group or club or shared activity, there may be a strong sense of belonging—stronger even than in your Christian experience. But does it nourish your soul and make you the person you want to become, the person God has created you to be?

Unfortunately, many of my friends who've left the faith haven't found what they were looking for. In search of freedom, they've found only bondage to a lifeless system of individualism, consumerism, and a new, secular judgmentalism. But those who've stayed when it's grown hard, or who've been hurt in the past but tried again in another community—they have often been so glad just a few years later.

We were made for this: belonging to Christ and one another. Every other system, every other promise, everything else in this world is crushing. Christianity's "secret ingredient" is its power of vibrant spiritual community worshiping Jesus Christ together. It takes years to build, sometimes decades. But find people who have given their life to building Christian fellowship and you'll see people who are connected, rooted, and thriving in Christ.

As for me, I'm deconstructing all right. I'm deconstructing this radical individualism I've inherited from my Western culture. I'm deconverting from this isolated way of life. I'm weary of the production-and-consumption treadmill.

Instead I'm looking for a more rooted, connected way of life. I want to be fully known and fully loved. I want a place to belong. I want to live for something bigger than myself; I want to find my life by giving it away; I want to build my community by laying down my immediate wants and desires.

In this sense, I'm heading off into the woods. I'm not looking for myself; I'm finding my people. I'm building my community, in a healthy church. You're welcome to join us.

14

SOMETIMES PEOPLE DON'T BELIEVE

JARED WILSON

I received the phone call from a concerned church member. Two relatives, a husband and wife, were both dying. "Would you please go share the gospel with them?" the member asked.

It wasn't the first time I'd received such a request. As the only evangelical pastor in a rural Vermont town, I'd been sent on plenty of evangelistic errands before, serving as the missionary by proxy for believers worried about the eternal state of their unbelieving loved ones. I can't think of a time I didn't comply. But this situation was a little different: a married couple, both on the verge of death. He was in the hospital; she was in a nursing home. I sat by their deathbeds and told them about Jesus.

The wife made a profession of faith. Her husband did not. "I've done my life without it," he said to me, implying it didn't make sense to change course now.

It was startling to me then, as it still is to me now. This spiritual contrast has haunted me in the years since. I didn't offer them different messages. My wording might have been slightly different, but the basic information was the same. The good news is the good news. And I would've thought that if any moment would be ripe for even a "what have I got to lose?" Pascal's wager, it would be on one's deathbed. But she believed. And he didn't.

Why?

WHERE DO WE PLACE THE WEIGHT OF BELIEF?

If you're deconstructing your faith, perhaps you have struggled with this reality. Or perhaps others, aware of your journey, have struggled with it. They may wonder how someone who grew up in the church, made a profession of faith, participated in the community of God, talked the talk, and walked the walk could now appear to be walking away. It's discouraging when those who grew up in the church or who've been otherwise exposed to the truth of Scripture, been ministered to well by Christians, and would appear to have every reason to believe nevertheless reject the faith. We don't always know what to do with that, do we?

I remember the early days of my discipleship, learning the ins and outs of evangelism, and the pressure applied on us to "seal the deal." We had to know all the apologetic angles, the right responses to objections, the savviest rhetorical maneuvers to win souls. The implication was that, if someone didn't believe, you did something wrong. The weight of belief was on the evangelist.

We may not train our churches in evangelism with an "always be closing" mentality anymore. But you can tell that many evangelicals still think the weight of belief falls on our evangelism by the ways we wring our hands about increasing deconstruction stories, how we contemplate the "ex-evangelical" phenomenon, and the like. If you're rethinking your commitment to the faith, there are likely friends and family members around you mulling over what exactly they did or didn't do that might have led you to this moment.

I read last year of yet another fairly prominent Christian celebrity announcing his deconstruction. Jon Steingard, lead singer of the CCM group Hawk Nelson, explained his decision this way: "After growing up in a Christian home, being a pastor's kid, playing and singing in a Christian band, and having the word 'Christian' in front of most of the things in my life, I am now finding that I no longer believe in God." I don't know anything about Steingard other than what he disclosed. I will take at face value his claims that his faith, such as it was, could not withstand the weight of his questions. The church certainly does face a discipleship deficit when we're not preparing our young people especially to apply the truths of Scripture to an increasingly "post-truth" culture.

But unlike many of my evangelical brethren, I don't feel an inordinate need to rush in and perform a spiritual autopsy in response to every deconstruction story.

To be clear, any time one who was raised in the church and who professed the faith rejects it, it's a tragedy worthy of serious contemplation and prayer. But we ought to be careful about reflexively grasping for easy answers.

And this goes for you too.

I noticed, in much of the social-media analyses of Steingard's announcement, a criticism of his childhood education, the quality of discipleship he received, and so on. I don't know how anybody who doesn't know the man, his family, or the churches of his raising—which apparently his father led—can make such arguments. I'd caution you about making such arguments, too.

Now, there is definitely a severe deficiency in the state of evangelical discipleship. In fact the dominant mode of discipleship in American evangelicalism facilitates this very result. So generally speaking, yes, the way Americans "do church" isn't great at training converts to plant deep spiritual roots, center their lives on the gospel, commit to a Christian community, and affirm the sufficiency of God's Word. We have by and large traded in robust spiritual formation according to the biblical gospel for superficial religious affirmation according to consumeristic moralism, so we shouldn't be surprised that more people from this system are rejecting traditional Christianity for a message of being true to yourself.

Maybe you did grow up in a church that didn't do justice to your searching questions, didn't act mercifully in relation to your doubts, and didn't respond in Christlike ways to your failings or of those of your friends and classmates. Maybe your church really did fail you. It happens.

And while looking for someone to pin our doubts on is completely understandable, the truth about how we come to believe—and disbelieve—is a lot more complicated than we often think. Easy answers about poor discipleship don't always fit.

We like the easy explanations. A professing Christian deconstructs? *He obviously didn't have a good preacher*, we think. A young man or woman rejects the faith? *They obviously didn't experience deep discipleship.*

Except sometimes they do. Maybe you did, too. During my decades in ministry, I've seen more than a few young people grow up in the church and out of the faith. Nearly all of them had loving parents who, though imperfect, did their best. I won't claim at all to have been a perfect pastor, but I've never led a church that treated doubters in graceless ways or utterly refused to answer their questions with compassion.

The truth is, sometimes people just don't believe.

SPIRITUAL ANSWERS TO INTELLECTUAL QUESTIONS

Paul warned his protégé about the reality of apostasy:

> Now the Spirit expressly says that in later times some will depart from the faith by devoting themselves to deceitful spirits and teachings of demons, through the insincerity of liars whose consciences are seared, who forbid marriage and require abstinence from foods that God created to be received with thanksgiving by those who believe and know the truth. (1 Tim. 4:1–3)

I notice a few things about this warning, all of which add up to an unavoidable conclusion. Paul "credits" departing from the faith to deceitful spirits, teachings of demons, insincerity of liars, and seared consciences. I know that if you're sorting out your commitment to the truth claims of Christianity, these sorts of arguments may not strike you as particularly convincing. If it's a wholesale rejection of theism or a spiritual worldview you're contemplating, hearing about the influence of demonic activity or the spirit world isn't likely a great persuader in rethinking your understanding of disbelief. But while these influences Paul mentions are manifested in particular teachings and laws particular to Timothy's context—heretical asceticism many of us in the West don't have to deal with very much (if at all) today—the bottom line of the apostasy is the same today as yesterday: people depart from the faith for spiritual reasons.

We tend to assign logical explanations to apparently inexplicable actions because we're pragmatists at heart. When Christians witness someone rejecting the gospel of Jesus, they often think they didn't give the right presentation, offer the best apologetic answers, and so on. And sometimes we do get in our own way. But the reality of the Holy Spirit resists such rationale.

This is why, for instance, for every person raised in the church only to reject the faith, there is another raised entirely outside the community of faith who against all odds decides to become a disciple of Jesus. We likely all know some unlikely converts—those raised in difficult, awful, even abusive environments, or simply environments where they were "discipled" not to care about the things of God—who have come to unlikely and astounding life by the power of the gospel.

Christianity, for all of its historical claims and intellectual content, is above all *supernatural*.

No matter the earthly means—a friend's testimony, a parent or Sunday-school teacher's counsel, a preacher's invitation, a tract or a book or a TV program or even a tweet—the difference between belief and unbelief is not in the presentation but in the Spirit's awakening presence. By grace God condescends to use human means (Rom. 10:14), but the power is his alone. Saving faith is a gift from God (Eph. 2:8).

JESUS'S TEACHING ON DISBELIEF

Do you remember that moment after Jesus's resurrection when he appears to his disciples? There is a precious interaction later between Thomas and our Lord that in a few words tells us a lot about the nature of belief. Because Thomas wasn't in the room, he hears the news with incredulity. "I won't believe," he basically says, "unless I can see and hear and touch" (John 20:25).

Maybe you feel you are in Thomas's position. You may not be sure if you can believe the Bible—or you're sure you don't—but you can identify with Thomas, can't you? The idea that Jesus has bodily risen from the dead just sounds so impossible. It defies what we know about reality. It would be a miracle unlike any ever seen before or since. When Thomas says he won't—*can't*—believe unless he sees, we feel it.

And we assume from Jesus's words that he deigns to let Thomas do just that. But he also makes it a point to say something astounding. Do you remember? "Have you believed because you have seen me?" Jesus says. "Blessed are those who have not seen and yet have believed" (John 20:29).

In a way, Jesus counters the notion that belief is an obvious response to credible evidence. His remarks to Thomas remind us that belief is fundamentally a spiritual matter. This is a parallel declaration to one of the major points of his story about Lazarus and the rich man in Luke 16:19–31. The latter, from the torments of Hades, begins to plead across the chasm with Abraham to raise Lazarus from the grave and send him as a miraculous sign to the rich man's unbelieving loved ones:

> And [the rich man] said, "Then I beg you, father, to send him to my father's house—for I have five brothers—so that he may warn them, lest they also come into this place of torment." But Abraham said, "They have Moses and the Prophets; let them hear them." And he said, "No, father Abraham, but if someone goes to them from the dead, they will repent." He said to him, "If they do not hear Moses and the Prophets, neither will they be convinced if someone should rise from the dead." (Luke 16:27–31)

Jesus, by way of Abraham, rebuts the notion that anyone would be-lieve simply by witnessing a miracle. Maybe you've said something just like that. "If God would just speak to me or show up somehow or prove himself, then of course I'd believe." But listen to Jesus's re-sponse. I know it's a hard word, but if you still have at the very least an admiration for him, pay attention to what he says: "No, you wouldn't."

If the Holy Spirit speaking through his living and active Scrip-ture doesn't change your heart from stone to flesh, Jesus is saying, no spectacular sign will do the trick. If one isn't changed by "Moses and the Prophets," even a miraculous resurrection won't change them. Paul says it this way in 1 Corinthians 1:22–25:

> For Jews demand signs and Greeks seek wisdom, but we preach
> Christ crucified, a stumbling block to Jews and folly to Gentiles, but to
> those who are called, both Jews and Greeks, Christ the power of God
> and the wisdom of God. For the foolishness of God is wiser than men,
> and the weakness of God is stronger than men.

The message is the power. And the difference between belief and un-belief is not ultimately a well-turned phrase, a withering argument, or even a compelling service. Nobody can ultimately make Christianity look good enough to plant faith in your heart. To be born again is a spiritual matter. There are lots of things Christians can do to adorn the power of God, but there's nothing we can do to enhance or replace it. According to Jesus, the difference between belief in him and rejection of him is a matter of the Spirit (Matt. 16:17; Luke 10:21).

I don't know Jon Steingard's story. He says he's open to experi-encing a revelation from God that changes his mind (back?). I hope that's true, and that the Lord answers his prayer. I don't know your story. Maybe you feel too far into deconstruction to turn back. You may think you've heard too little or been hurt too much to maintain the faith you once claimed.

But we have to remember that sometimes people don't believe not because they didn't hear the right answers, but because they heard them only with their minds and not with their hearts. And by that, I don't mean they were never emotionally invested in the things of faith. Many deconversion stories in fact include lots of details about how much the unbeliever once "really believed." It's a delicate matter to suss out, but it's important for us to remember that a sense of belonging, an emotional investment, and even a religious fervency do not equate to spiritual regeneration.

In his public statement, Steingard posited some weak intellectual objections common among those who think superficially about the truth claims of Christian theism. So maybe he wasn't discipled well, after all. Or maybe he was, and he just doesn't believe. Sometimes people just don't believe.

WHAT IF I'M NOT ELECT?

What do we do then? What should you do if you or those you love still want to walk away from Jesus?

Because Christians pray, we acknowledge that God has power that we don't. The call and impulse to prayer ought to remind us daily that the kind of change we are looking for—in us, in others, in the world—can only be empowered by the sovereign Lord himself. He may use articulate proclamations, compelling witness, and thoughtful apologetics, but ultimately what people need only he can provide by his gracious power.

In terms of the salvation of the lost—whether converted or "deconverted"—it means that we shouldn't move on from the gospel. A member of my last church came to saving faith in a previous church after attending services there for more than a year. He started taking his family to church each Sunday because he considered it a good thing to do. *Good people go to church*, he thought. By his own account, he heard the gospel every week at this faithful church. But it was one particular Sunday after he'd logged 52 Sundays hearing the message that it occurred to him, "Hey, *I* need to believe this!"

Sometimes people grow to faith gradually through patient handholding and meticulous answers to their objections and explanations of their confusions. I recall Don Carson telling a story about a young man he led to the Lord after a series of weeknight meetings answering apologetic questions. By all outward appearances, this young man was effectively "argued into" the kingdom. But the reality for his conversion was the same as for that man in my church. The Spirit at his appointed time awakened their hearts to believe. God's elect were effectively called. The circumstances of the call may look different person to person, culture to culture, but the difference-maker is always the same. The gospel of a sovereign God is the power of belief (Rom. 1:16).

What about you? Maybe you're on the verge of chucking the whole thing in the wastebasket. Or maybe you're just struggling with the question of your salvation. How do you know you really believe? If all this talk of the Spirit making the true difference is itself true, how can you know you're saved?

First, I have not known many unsaved persons to worry about salvation. The fact that you'd be concerned about whether you're elect is a good sign that you are. It's likely evidence of a softened heart, which is itself evidence of the Spirit's work in you.

Second, however, I would say that the desire for salvation is itself the initial sign of the gospel's work. And if you genuinely choose Jesus, you can be sure it is because he has chosen you. The danger of disbelief could not be greater. It is indeed eternal conscious torment in the place called hell. But those who come to Jesus in faith need not have a strong faith or even a totally knowledgeable faith—just a *true* faith. It can be small. It can be weak. It can be battered. Because it is not a strong faith that saves, but a strong Savior. And if you want him, it's because he wants you. And we have the promise that anyone who comes to him will never be rejected (John 6:37).

If you're weary, wavering, wondering, and wandering into the realm of unbelief, keep looking to the person of Jesus in Scripture, and don't look away.

15

TAKE A HARD LOOK AT JESUS

DEREK RISHMAWY

If you've come to the end of this book, you're either thinking about deconstructing your faith or you're worried about how to talk to folks who are. Deconstruction processes aren't detached exercises in pure reason—they're inevitably personal, messy, and uncomfortable.

While I haven't had a full-blown "I can't believe this anymore" moment, over the years I've endured seasons of doubt when I pulled it all apart, bit by bit, anxious to see if it could be pieced together again.

My two pieces of advice—or rather, my argument—is, first, as you walk down this road, approach it intentionally. Don't just let it "happen" to you. Second, you need a guide, something or someone to help you focus on what really matters. I can think of none better to fill that role than Jesus himself—his words, his actions, and his person.

I suppose that's an intuitive, Sunday-school point: focus on Christ to figure out what you believe about Christianity. What does that mean, though? First, there is the content issue—what should I spend time examining? What issues do I need to wrestle with, and where do I start? And second, how do I approach this process honestly?

Jesus guides us through all three stages of every deconstruction I've seen: the issues, the issues *underneath* the issues, and the Big Issue.

JESUS AND THE ISSUES

Whenever I read about someone deconstructing the faith, usually a predictable (and legitimate) package of issues tends to come up: the authority of the Bible considering history and science, miracles, evolution, and so forth. Then there are moral issues like Old Testament violence, or the Bible's perspective on sexuality or women. Finally, I can't tell you how often I have heard that "the church," a particular church, or a pastor has failed and wounded a Christian in such a way that the entire experience of faith may seem unreal.

Several of the other essays in this book have tackled those questions directly. My main point here is that as much as possible, you should pay attention to Jesus himself—his concrete words and deeds in the Gospels—as you struggle.

DON'T FAN-FIC JESUS, LISTEN TO HIM

What do I mean?

It's easy to create a fan-fiction Jesus. Folks grab onto a single thread, transform it, and build it into a vague abstraction of Jesus as the avatar of loving, accepting inclusivity or hostility to "religion." Suddenly, we're posting memes about what Jesus would *really* say if he were here today, oblivious to how they contradict the actual statements he made. (Perhaps you're even reacting to someone's fan-fiction Jesus in the process!) Appealing to the "spirit of Jesus" for our newfound discomfort with Christianity, we can miss the inconvenient fact that our problem isn't just with Christianity but Christ himself.

Before you end up down that road, read Jesus's words and watch his deeds in the Gospels.

Read his woes against the religious leaders and recognize that there's never been a fiercer critic of hypocritical, false, and distorted faith that perverts the Scriptures for power, authority, and money (Luke 6; Matt. 23). Behold the Jesus who fiercely condemns those who cause little ones to stumble in their faith through abuse or false teaching (Matt. 18:6).[1]

But then keep reading and see that Jesus's critique of perverse, merely human religious traditions stems from his unique authority as the Messiah, or by appeal to a correct interpretation of the Old Testament (Matt. 15:1–9; 22:29–33; 23:2–3; Mark 7:1–13; John 5:39–47). Jesus declares not an iota will pass away from the Law (Matt. 5:18), for Scripture is the "word of God" that "cannot be broken" (John 10:35). Contrary to certain contemporary trends, Jesus's challenge to "bad religion" is driven by a high regard for God's Word.

Read on to see the Jesus who accepts tax collectors and sinners (Mark 2:14–17). Watch him deal gently with the woman at the well with five husbands (John 4) and welcome the notoriously sinful woman who had "loved much" (Luke 7:36–50). But when asked about divorce, this same Jesus takes a hardline, "conservative" stance on the matter. Citing God's creation of male and female in his image, their complementarity, and God's intent for their permanent union on the basis of Genesis 1–2, he says that many remarriages are adultery (Mark 10:1–12). Jesus magnifies both mercy and God's moral law.

Christ is the gracious Lord who forbids us to hate our enemies or return evil for evil, because our kind God makes the rain shine on the just and unjust (Matt. 5:38–48). He also threatens hellfire for those who ignore his words (Matt. 5:22; 10:28; 23:33). He claims the whole Old Testament testifies to himself and his gospel (Luke 24:27; John 5:39), but he doesn't bat an eye in referencing the judgment of the flood (Matt. 24:37) or the destruction of Sodom and Gomorrah (Luke 17:26–32).

We could continue, but as you rethink the faith in view of Jesus, never lose sight of the actual, concrete person of Jesus from the only witnesses we have. Which brings me to the issues *underneath* the is-

---

1.   On all of this, see John Wenham, *Christ and the Bible*, 3rd ed. (Eugene, OR: Wipf and Stock, 2009), 16–68.

sues. Like an iceberg, there's usually more going on beneath the surface of any doctrinal deconstruction.

JESUS AND THE ISSUES UNDER THE ISSUES

In college, I had a friend in the philosophy program with whom I argued frequently. He was an atheist, and I was the token Christian in class. Unsurprisingly, we debated the existence of God, Jesus, and so forth. One day I finally asked him, "If I could come up with answers to all of your objections, would you even *want* to believe?" (I'd heard my pastor say he'd tried this once, so I gave it a shot.) He stopped, looked at me, and said, "You know, probably not. Deep down I think I don't like the idea of someone telling me what to do with my life." Quite the self-aware 20 year old.

Our minds are never disconnected from our hearts. Dealing honestly with that tie is crucial for reconstructing our faith. Engaging our intellectual and moral doubts is never a dispassionate, purely rational process. We're motivated reasoners, believers, and doubters. We're emotional thinkers.

Once again, Jesus can help us.

JESUS, HEART-SOIL INSPECTOR

Jesus tells a parable about seeds sown in four soils, to explain the varied reactions to his message of the kingdom (Mark 4:1–20). Some reject his message because Satan snatches the seed from their heart. Others give a shallow response because they have a shallow grasp; having no root, they're unprepared to hold on during trial and persecution. Meanwhile, others let the word be choked out by "the cares of the world and the deceitfulness of riches and the desire for other things."

Believers can hang on to teachings for bad-faith reasons: they fear losing face in their family or community, or they're comfortably ensconced in networks in which their beliefs reinforce social power. Perhaps the sins to which they're tempted are socially acceptable, so they only deal with a manageable level of guilt and shame. This isn't robust faith—it's self-deceit.

At the same time, Jesus warns that we can balk at his Word amid all sorts of emotional drives and social pressures that we haven't wanted to acknowledge, even to ourselves. It's worth thinking through some ways these hidden motives or external pressures work in the soil of our hearts.

MONEY, SEX, AND COMFORT

Jesus is blunt about basic reasons like money, sex, and comfort. Recall the rich young ruler who walks away from Jesus dismayed, unwilling to give away his possessions (Mark 10:17–27). I've been doing college ministry long enough to see that while many come by their doubts honestly, it's not a coincidence that others become skeptical right around the time their extracurricular activities start conflicting with their prior moral convictions. Other students mysteriously let their faith slide when their career begins to take off. Obviously, that is not everybody—and it may not be you—but Jesus forces us to reckon with the fact that it's at least *some* of us.

From another angle, several high-profile deconstructed Christians have mentioned changing their views on sexuality and gender to LGBT+ affirmation once they began to interact with LGBT+ folks. Some realized they lacked deep theological convictions about creation or the nature of male, female, and marriage, and merely held instinctive, mean-spirited prejudices. Others saw in folks a humanity they hadn't acknowledged before, causing them to reevaluate their theological positions—on all sorts of issues—out of a desire to love them better.

No doubt that is some of what happened. But Jesus also leads us to ask, is it *only* a newfound respect and love for others that leads us to take action on these questions? Couldn't there also be a layer of fear of disapproval, as you enter a new community whose good opinion begins to matter more to you? Couldn't there also be a desire to avoid "the tribulation and persecution" that "arises on account of the word" (Mark 4:17)? Nobody wants to feel unloving—to lose friends, to knowingly cause pain with words or beliefs. Nobody wants to be (or be called) a bigot, to face the stares in the office—much less an awkward and potentially costly conversation with the HR representative.

Jesus forces us to be honest about the pressures we face.

POWER OF NARRATIVES AND THE CAMP TESTIMONY EFFECT

Deconstruction is even easier when you consider there is a ready-made, moral narrative you can make your own. Sociologists and philosophers have been telling us for decades that we think of our lives in terms of stories, dramas, and scripts, more often than not taking them from our surrounding culture and fitting the events of our lives within them.[2] Our faith journeys are no different.

The philosopher Charles Taylor notes that since the 1800s there has been a common script of intellectual shift as a "coming of age." Doubting the faith you inherited from your parents becomes a heroic step into intellectual adulthood and maturity.[3] In our own age, embracing an allegedly humble uncertainty instead of harsh dogmatism is praiseworthy. If you can do that in the name of inclusive justice or love of neighbor, so much the better for your relative sense of righteousness. Indeed, it might even be worth the persecution of your old church community if it reinforces your identification with a new community that has become more important.

Another recognizable narrative is the post-evangelical or ex-evangelical account of fleeing harsh, dogmatic, abusive, and repressive church communities. I've been around churches long enough to know that too many of those stories are *true*—church trauma is real. What's more, Jesus knows it. He condemns those who "tie up heavy burdens, hard to bear, and lay them on people's shoulders" even as they are unwilling to lift a finger to help (Matt. 23:4). Pastors, be like Jesus and take these stories seriously and listen patiently. And if you've suffered church trauma, please, do not be ashamed to seek out a licensed counselor. Emotional healing is essential to spiritual healing.

Nevertheless, I've also seen what we might call the "camp testimony" effect. If you've been to a youth camp, you might remember those nights when folks share testimonies about struggling with sin, repenting, and embracing forgiveness in Christ. One kid stands and tells a personal story, opening a floodgate of others. Over time you

---

2.   See Christian Smith, *Moral Believing Animals: Human Personhood and Culture* (Oxford: Oxford University Press, 2003).

3.   Charles Taylor, *A Secular Age* (Cambridge, MA: Harvard University Press, 2007), 560–66.

notice the way the first story shapes the way the next is told. If your testimony lacks that pathos, then a little reinterpreting to strengthen it can help. It's often not even intentional—we really begin to remember things that way.

Of course, the camp-testimony effect can happen in reverse. Old experiences, even beliefs, are transfigured and re-narrated to explain a break with faith. Therapists point out that many couples approaching divorce do something similar. When their relationship is frustrating enough, they rewrite its early days as well; serious troubles in the present retroactively render it a "loveless marriage" from the start.[4] The temptation is to do the same with Jesus, especially when there is a popular deconstruction template ready at hand. As more folks re-narrate their faith experiences, it becomes an increasingly powerful explanatory grid and self-replicating process.[5] None of this means there isn't an issue—there probably is. It just means we need to be critically aware of the way other stories shape our own.

We could walk through more scenarios, but this is enough to prompt us to consider the warning in the alternate narrative Jesus gives us in the parable. Approaching deconstruction in an intellectually honest way means facing our secret motives and the other influences at work alongside our reasoning about Jesus.

---

4. John M. Gottmann and Nan Silver, *The Seven Principles for Making Marriage Work: A Practical Guide from the Country's Foremost Relationship Expert* (New York: Three Rivers Press, 1999), 42–44.

5. Jason Blakely has recently discussed the "Double-H" effect ("double hermeneutic"), whereby popularized economic and social scientific models offered to explain human behavior end up filtering out into popular consciousness and "actually produce new identities, practices, and worlds of meaning." Jason Blakely, *We Built Reality: How Social Science Infiltrated Culture, Politics, and Power* (Oxford: Oxford University Press, 2020), xxvi. Put simply, the more popular economists talked about decisions in terms of the "rational consumer," and this mode of analyzing decision-making filtered out into the popular consciousness, the more folks started imagining themselves and their decisions in a consumeristic fashion, which then "confirms" the originally postulated thesis. The description and analysis contribute to the phenomenon. I'm suggesting something similar happens with our narratives of broken faith and deconstruction. Positing the narrative can recolor and reshape our experience from normal doubts and disappointments into shattered faith and absolute betrayals.

JESUS IS THE ISSUE

In the end, *Jesus* is the issue. We all face the question he posed to his disciples: "Who do you say that I am?" (Matt. 16:15). They rattled off the popular options: John the Baptist, Elijah, Jeremiah, or one of the other prophets. But Jesus wanted to know, "What about you?" To which Peter replied, "You are the Messiah, the Son of the living God" (Matt. 16:16).

Can you say the same? Take care, though—folks "believe in Jesus" in all sorts of ways. They believe Jesus the good-but-not-quite-perfect-and-therefore-correctable Teacher. Jesus the pretty insightful Adviser. Jesus the conveniently malleable Symbol of the Moment.

No, who did *he* claim to be? Is he the great Son of Man with authority to forgive sins (Mark 2:10)? The "I am" who exists from eternity (John 8:58)? The way, the truth, and the life through whom alone we can reach the Father (John 14:6)? The perfect one whom nobody can accuse of sin (John 8:46)? Is he the Lord who claims all authority in heaven and on earth and has been vindicated in the resurrection by the Father (Matt. 28:18; Rom. 8:11)? The One who says that to love him is to obey him and keep his commandments (John 14:15)? Is he the Crucified One, who gave his life as a ransom for you (Mark 10:45)? The question is whether we trust him on his terms—if not, then don't trust him at all. If Jesus is who he says he is, then he is trustworthy, so you can rely on him to patiently help you sort out the rest. If he isn't, then none of it is worth worrying about anyway.

Don't misunderstand me. Taking a hard look at Jesus can cut in several directions. It may mean leaving an abusive church. It may reshuffle your politics. It may lead to some weird, uncertain places for a time—I ended up a Presbyterian! But at least you'll make a clear-eyed decision about the choice before you.

When you approach this deconstruction, it may be tempting to let yourself to treat life with Christ as an abstract set of doctrines, an institution, or a brand to associate with. Don't depersonalize it. To quote the classic hymn, "Turn your eyes upon Jesus, look full in his wonderful face." I don't promise the things of earth will grow strangely dim, but in light of Jesus—his grace, his power, his compassion, his glory—everything else will take on proper perspective.

In the person of Jesus, those hungering for righteousness see his justice. Those thirsty for compassion see One who will not break a bent reed. Those battling doubt meet One who hears prayers to help our unbelief without judgment or shame. And those perplexed with confusion over the complexities of life, and the fear of being lied to yet again, come face to face with the only One who is faithful and true.

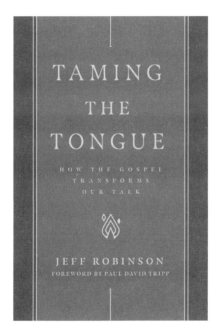

"This book hit home with me, perhaps because some of my greatest regrets have come from ways I've misused words—confidences I didn't keep, criticism I was too eager to offer, bragging to make myself seem important, dominating the conversation when I should have listened. I've also misused words by keeping silent when I should have come clean, when I should have offered praise, when I should have spoken up. These and many more insights on how we use our words are covered in this brief but wisdom-filled book—a great book to read prayerfully on your own, but even better to use to discuss with a small group."

NANCY GUTHRIE, author and Bible teacher

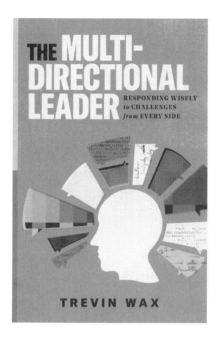

"Trevin Wax writes with keenness of insight, pastoral wisdom, and prophetic forcefulness. In this book he articulates the pressure today's Christian leaders feel from every direction. Wax remains one of my most reliable counselors for leading in a rapidly shifting context."

J. D. GREEAR, pastor, The Summit Church, Raleigh-Durham, North Carolina; president, Southern Baptist Convention

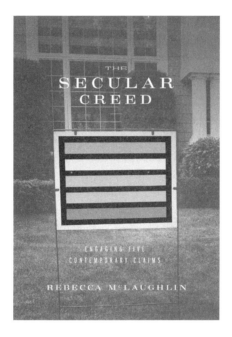

"In this book, Rebecca McLaughlin offers a gentle, yet powerful biblical corrective that calls readers to holistic Christian love—a higher calling than the call of the culture, and, often, a harder calling. She examines popular cultural mantras and answers each one with the truth and application of the gospel of Christ. In her balanced and gracious approach, she paints our culture's arguments in the most compassionate light possible—and then shows the beauty of a more excellent way!"

JASMINE HOLMES, author of *Mother to Son: Letters to a Black Boy on Identity and Hope*

TGC THE GOSPEL COALITION

The Gospel Coalition (TGC) supports the church in making disciples of all nations, by providing gospel-centered resources that are trusted and timely, winsome and wise.

Guided by a Council of more than 40 pastors in the Reformed tradition, TGC seeks to advance gospel-centered ministry for the next generation by producing content (including articles, podcasts, videos, courses, and books) and convening leaders (including conferences, virtual events, training, and regional chapters).

In all of this we want to help Christians around the world better grasp the gospel of Jesus Christ and apply it to all of life in the 21st century. We want to offer biblical truth in an era of great confusion. We want to offer gospel-centered hope for the searching.

Join us by visiting TGC.org so you can be equipped to love God with all your heart, soul, mind, and strength, and to love your neighbor as yourself.